creating ART with BREAD DOUGH

by Dona Z. Meilach

photographs by
Mel and Dona Meilach

CROWN PUBLISHERS, INC., NEW YORK

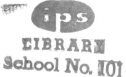

Dedicated to my editor Brandt Aymar
and the entire staff at Crown Publishers

Inquiries should be addressed to Crown Publishers, Inc.,
One Park Avenue, New York, N.Y. 10016.
Printed in the United States of America
Published simultaneously in Canada by
General Publishing Company Limited

Designed by Laurie Zuckerman

Library of Congress Cataloging in Publication Data

Meilach, Dona Z.
    Creating art with bread dough.

  Bibliography: p.
  Includes index.
    1. Bread dough craft. I. Meilach, Mel.
II. Title.
TT880.M43 1976   745.5   76-8944
ISBN 0-517-52589-5
ISBN 0-517-52590-9 pbk.

Third Printing, April, 1978

Contents

Other arts and crafts books by Dona Z. Meilach

Fibers and Fabrics

CONTEMPORARY BATIK AND TIE-DYE
CONTEMPORARY LEATHER
CREATING ART FROM FIBERS AND FABRICS
CREATIVE STITCHERY with Lee Erlin Snow
MACRAME ACCESSORIES
MACRAME: CREATIVE DESIGN IN KNOTTING
MAKING CONTEMPORARY RUGS AND WALL HANGINGS
A MODERN APPROACH TO BASKETRY with Fibers and Grasses
SOFT SCULPTURE and Other Soft Art Forms
WEAVING OFF-LOOM with Lee Erlin Snow

Sculpture

CONTEMPORARY ART WITH WOOD
CONTEMPORARY STONE SCULPTURE
CREATING MODERN FURNITURE
CREATING SMALL WOOD OBJECTS AS FUNCTIONAL SCULPTURE
CREATING WITH PLASTER
CREATIVE CARVING
DIRECT METAL SCULPTURE
SCULPTURE CASTING with Dennis Kowal

Collage-Paper

ACCENT ON CRAFTS
BOX ART: Assemblage and Construction
COLLAGE AND ASSEMBLAGE with Elvie Ten Hoor
CREATING ART FROM ANYTHING
PAPERCRAFT
PAPIER-MÂCHÉ ARTISTRY
PRINTMAKING

Design

THE ARTIST'S EYE
HOW TO CREATE YOUR OWN DESIGNS with Jay and Bill Hinz

Also

THE ART OF BELLY DANCING with Dahlena

Acknowledgments

Nothing could be further from the truth than the old adage "Too many cooks spoil the broth" when it comes to creating art forms with bread dough. Interviews with artists proved that a more apt cliché should be "the more the merrier." Each artist brought a new set of ideas and experiences to the expressive potential of the medium. I am indebted to all who generously shared their working methods and findings.

My special thanks to Maureen Talbott, San Diego, California, whose adult-education classroom became a research center for testing ideas and checking methods reported by others. Maureen helped to experiment with innovative techniques and finishes. When I needed corroboration of my own results, she would exhaust the possible pros and cons through additional testing.

Virginia Black, Studio City, California, one of today's outstanding dough artists and dollmaker, gladly demonstrated her simple and sure methods of creating adorable, whimsical objects. Kay Whitcomb, La Jolla, California, spent a day developing her special techniques before our cameras. Both gave us carte blanche to use examples from their vast collections. Thank you, thank you.

Thanks too to Bernice A. Houston, Chula Vista, California, who phoned and asked, "What can I do to help?" exactly at the point when an experienced hand was needed to work up the series for the bread and glue recipe in chapter 3. She was, indeed, manna from heaven.

Ruby Chambers of Evansville, Indiana, phoned to find out what the book would include, then had other craftsmen contact me. I am especially grateful to Ruby's daughter, Linda Fugate, Northboro, Massachusetts, for sending her absolutely incredible miniature sculptured figurines that are more delicate than Dresden china. I probably would not have believed they were made of bread dough had I not actually handled and photographed them myself.

I recall the pleasant trip from Chicago to Ogden Dunes, Indiana, where we photographed the works of Lois Crachy and Arlene Seitzinger. When Arlene, whose media are normally stone, wood, wax, and clay, became intrigued with the possibilities of bread dough, she attacked the medium with enthusiasm. Her results probably are unlike anything known to bread dough before . . . since the beginning of time.

Thank you Marian and Ted Gault, Sunnyvale, California, and Barbara Herberholz, Carmichael California, and Valerie Anne Smith, Great Falls, Montana, for the excellent demonstrations and photographs that you sent.

I am most appreciative to the scores of artists who shipped their pieces from all over the country to be photographed and to those who submitted photographs. Only space limitations prevented use of all the excellent examples.

My gratitude to Robert Rothschild, President, and Gus Leep, Vice-President, of Illinois Bronze Powder and Paint Co., Lake Zurich, Illinois, for their technical advice about paints and finishes.

I must acknowledge my family's help who, at various times, became involved in some way. Susan, visiting from Richmond, Virginia, worked with me, and the result was an approach that no one else had reported. Allen, a graduate architectural student home from college for the summer, tugged at half a recipe and created the Art Deco figure in chapter 5 so his favorite period in art history design would be represented and, at the same time, developed another potential for the medium.

As always, my husband, Mel, was my indispensable photographic associate. I cannot recall how often he smiled sickly but with stoical patience when, though I had been baking all day, I announced we would have to go out for supper because there was nothing to eat.

I am grateful to Visual Productions, Inc., San Diego, California, for their excellent photographic processing. And I am awed by the expertise with which Collette Russell helped with correspondence and deciphered my drafts into a perfectly typed manuscript.

DONA MEILACH
San Diego, California

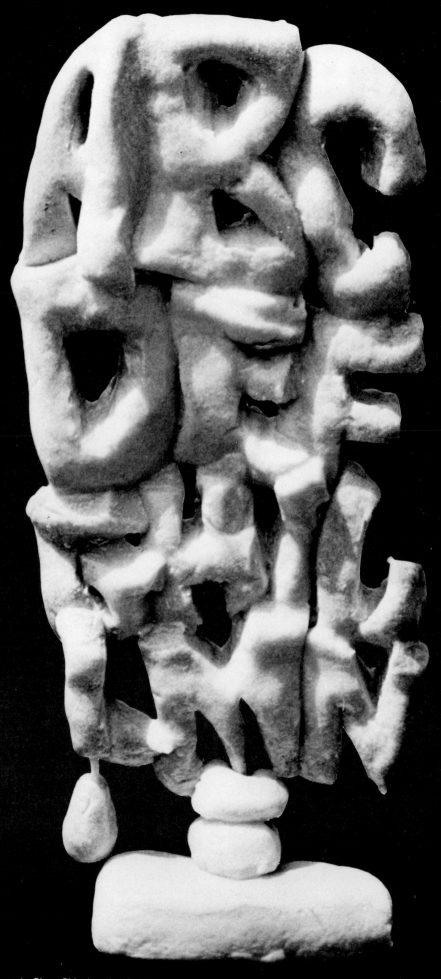

Homage to Claes Oldenburg's "Soft Ice Cream
Bar." By Dona Meilach. 8″ high, 4½″ wide.

1
HOW BREAD BECAME AN ART MEDIUM

Considering the centuries that peoples have been baking and forming bread in countless ways, it would seem nearly impossible that there would still be unexplored directions for such a basic substance to take. Considering also that people have created art almost from the beginning of time, one would have to stretch the imagination tremendously to believe that bread could find a new place among contemporary art media. Yet, both of these "impossibilities" are happening today: changing the recipe of edible bread or adding glues to baked bread results in an artistic medium whose potentials are only beginning to be explored.

There is no written history that pinpoints the origins of the recipes used to make the art objects shown throughout this book. A woman in her eighties explained that she had used a similar dough when she was a girl but that the pieces never held up; they were only child's play. The use of the inedible flour, water, and salt recipe called "baker's clay," which, when baked, becomes incredibly hard, has possibly been employed by peoples of many cultures, but the lack of preservative finishes has precluded any permanency. If any objects made from the mixture were found in ancient civilizations, archaeologists have not detected them. More likely, bread was baked by early peoples strictly for consumption; even ritual breads were baked of edible recipes.

The first chronicled acknowledgment of bread dough used as baker's clay by artists as a sculptural material appeared in an exhibition presented by the Museum of Contemporary Crafts of the American Craftsmen's Council in 1965. Even then, the objects made were whimsical, almost like an afterthought to the original intent of the show, which was to portray various forms of breads and cookies of different cultures. Possibly Jolyon Hofsted, a ceramist, who exhibited such items as a gin bottle of baker's clay or a shoe, was simply using the medium as another way to express the emerging Pop Art influence. When sculptor John Fischer exhibited a wounded bread with a bandage, and a bread on wheels, he was going beyond creating a decorative form to enhance a folk tradition. His pieces were subsequently exhibited in a New York art gallery.

Despite a rich and varied history of shaped breads, cookies, cakes, and candies in most cultures, mainly the Ecuadorians and Mexicans have evidenced pieces made to be permanent and inedible. Ecuadorian bread dolls depict figures with which the people are familiar: highly decorative shepherds, peasants, llamas, and other animals. Originally, they were made as cookies with icing; then, somehow, they were made so they would last. Today they are created from precolored nonedible bread doughs with great detail and in large and small pieces. They are valued as tourist and collector's items. Many are made assembly-line fashion with each person involved an expert at the type of trimmings applied: basic shaping, flowers, musical instruments, and hand painting.

In Mexico one finds delicate jewelry made into flowers and fashioned into brooches. It is these pieces that probably inspired people today to create miniatures used in egg decorating, dollhouses, and small dioramas that are enjoying great popularity.

The recipe used by the Mexicans, called "migajón," is not baked; it has been adapted by craftsmen with modern materials so that the basic ingre-

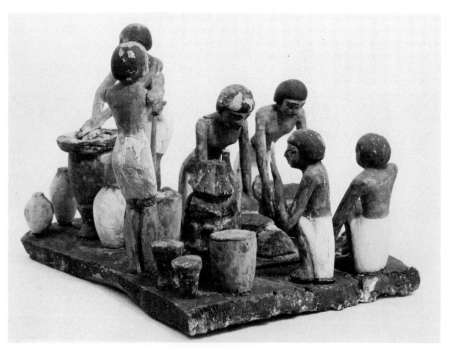

Wooden model of Egyptian bakers at work: c. 2000–1788 B.C. Figures are grinding, kneading, shaping, and baking loaves of bread with vessels for water and flour. *(Courtesy, The Oriental Institute, The University of Chicago, Chicago)*

dient—bread—is combined with white glue. The Mexicans, for as long as they have been making their miniature flowers, undoubtedly had other hardening materials before the introduction of modern glues.

The most innovative project with bread dough by a sculptor today is the bronze fountain at the front entrance of the Hyatt Hotel on Union Square in San Francisco installed in 1970. How is bread dough involved in a bronze fountain? Sculptor Ruth Asawa, the mother of six children, was always interested in keeping small hands busy. Through a series of professional experiences she evolved the idea of casting a bread-dough model in bronze using the same procedure known for centuries as "lost wax casting." She discovered that bread dough would burn out in much the same way as wax and the mold could be filled with bronze—hence bronze casting from a bread-dough original, or "lost bread-dough casting."

Chuck Basset, the architect for the Hyatt Hotel, and Ruth Asawa devised a plan for creating the fountain. The subject matter would include a folk art approach to the city of San Francisco. The panels were developed by young and old artists and nonartists. They depict anything and everything from the famed cable cars to pictures of Superman. A tour around the drum-shape fountain shows City Hall, the Ferry Building, Golden Gate Park, and well-known statues and landmarks. One point Ruth Asawa emphasizes is that the fountain was produced by many hands and, like all great folk monuments, it belongs to everyone everywhere.

The project was tremendous, involving 1,400 pounds of flour and salt. The ½-inch-thick pieces for each panel were rolled out and glued to a backing to prevent shrinkage. As the panels were drying, pieces of dough were rolled, flattened, squeezed, and pinched into shapes, and stuck down with white glue. The dough was not baked; rather, the panels were set aside to thoroughly dry out before being taken to the foundry for casting. During the rainy season, the salt in the dough absorbed moisture from the air, often causing the dough to spread or melt.

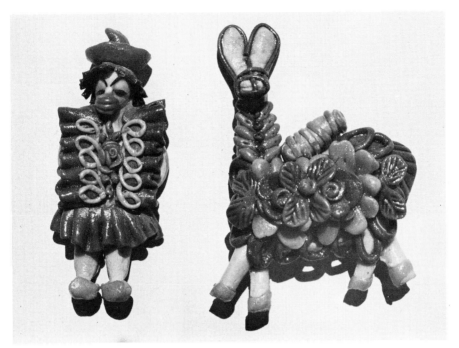

Ecuadorian bread-dough figures are highly glazed and brilliantly colored.

Ruth Asawa's popularization of the medium and the subsequent publicity enticed other people to experiment with bread dough. Craft magazines and craft pages of women's magazines offered the recipe and suggestions for simple objects that could be created with it. From all this the bread basket eventually evolved—a basket woven with strips of bread dough, baked and sealed with varnishes that would render the material permanent so that moisture would not permeate and thereby prevent organisms that tend to form mold in moist flour from growing. Undoubtedly, the development and use of polyurethane varnishes and plastic resins have been among the greatest spurs to the art of bread dough. Varnish, properly applied in several thin coats to seal bread-dough pieces, could conceivably enable them to last for years. Who knows what future archaeologists will unearth or how they will categorize their findings?

With all the new advances in materials and the emerging popularity of the medium, it is interesting to observe that the precedent for formed objects in the baker's medium is still deeply embedded in tradition.

Breadmaking dates back to the European Stone Age. Breads of many shapes were found in Egyptian tomb paintings dating from 1500 B.C. and possibly earlier. Some were shaped in cones and placed on altars. Others were formed as fish, birds, or mammals; many were colored with earth pigments and sprinkled with seed.

Before coins were invented, loaves of bread, along with beer and grain, were used in Egypt as payment for services. (Perhaps today's hip jargon with "bread" as the word for money hearkens back to this point in time.) From early documents and pictorial representations archaeologists concluded that bread acquired religious significance as it became an important food and was offered to the gods as a sacrifice just as earlier hunting peoples had offered game or wild fruits.

The most obvious evidence of the importance of bread comes from the Old and New Testaments in such concepts as "manna from heaven," "the Bread

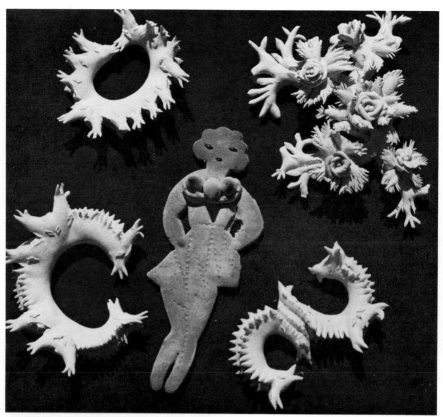

The center figure of a three-breasted doll of gingerbread from Frascati, Italy, is a local symbol of fertility. The others are "pane del Sardo," or Sardinian wedding breads, made on a couple's wedding day to symbolize union. *(Courtesy, Collection of the Hand and the Spirit, Crafts Gallery, Scottsdale, Arizona)*

of Life," and "the Miracle of the Loaves and Fishes." In translation from the Hebrew, Bethlehem, Christ's birthplace, means "House of Bread."

By the fifth century B.C., the Greeks had public bakeries. They also had elaborate religious beliefs; and devotees to the grain goddess, Demeter, brought offerings of wheat and honey cakes, some in the shape of plows.

The Romans acquired breads, leavened and unleavened, from earlier cultures, and the historian Pliny (A.D. 62–114) described the Roman breads as being made of wheat, millet, and broad bean flour; loaves were often in the form of fingers and wedding rings. Some were decorated with nuts, raisins, and sesame seeds. Bread stamps—beautifully designed from clay, wood, or metal, either molded or carved—were used to distinguish a baker's wares to guard bread from theft (the same reason a cattleman brands his cattle). Stamps were also made with religious symbols and used in Eucharistic breads.

Cookies baked in iron molds with geometric designs resembling those on some modern cookies have been recovered from sand-buried outposts in Chinese Turkestan from about A.D. 600–800.

Medieval Europe had a great local diversity of breads in terms of size, shape, and quality. Fancy breads, pies, and tarts were baked for fairs and religious holidays, some in animal or human forms as well as in twists, wreaths, and crescents. Some forms of special breads probably had their origins in pagan rituals, and those in human or animal shapes may once have been substitutes for actual human and animal sacrifices.

In medieval Europe the increase of towns and cities gave rise to commercial bakeries. The importance of bread is indicated by the derivations of two

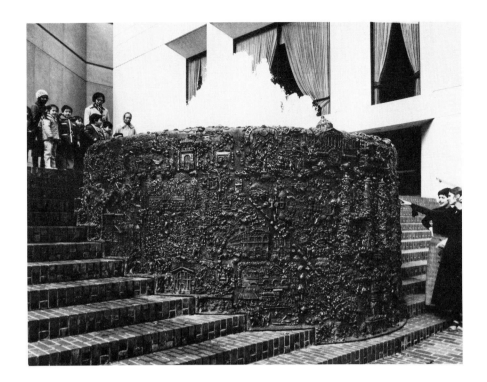

Ruth Asawa's Fountain on the Plaza, Hyatt on
Union Square, San Francisco. The bronze
drum-shape fountain was cast from bread-
dough panels created by young and old, artists
and nonartists, and depicts scenes of San Francisco. *Below:* Detail. *(Courtesy, Hyatt on Union
Square, San Francisco)*

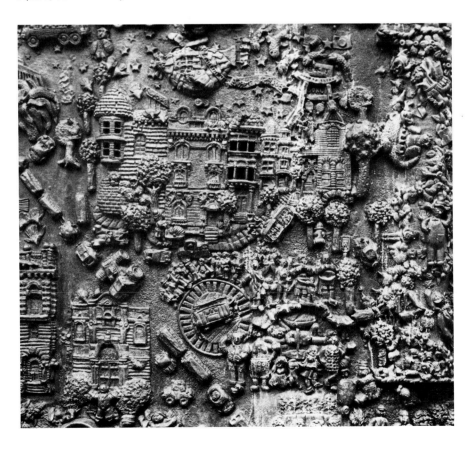

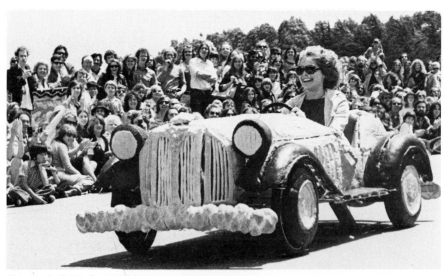

"Moulton's Edible Special." By Dorcas Moulton. Made of 100 pounds white and Russian rye bread for "The First Artists' Soap Box Derby" sponsored by the San Francisco Museum of Art, 1975. The piece was eaten after the race. *(Photo, Jan Butterfield)*

common Anglo-Saxon words descriptive of medieval life, "lord" and "lady." "Lord" is literally "loafward" or "breadkeeper," and "lady" is "loaf-servant" or "breadmaker." Our word "loaf," now referring to a shaped mass of the final baked product, was originally a general word for bread.

The history of grain and bread is closely and curiously linked to several events in history. For example, dissatisfactions with bread were among the grievances leading to the French Revolution; during the Revolution a bread dole like one in ancient Rome was set up in Paris. With the coming of Napoleon I, steps were taken in France to improve bread quality and stabilize prices.

The breads and cookies of European countries were considerably more elaborate and ritualistic than those of Near Eastern and Islamic countries, and few of the staple grains of China and the Orient could really be classified as cookies. Therefore, ritual and festive breads and cookies as a baker's art have their heritage in European cultures.

A cameolike pale cookie baked of a nonrising dough called Springerle (its recipe is in many cookbooks) is an old German and Swiss tradition. It is impressed with an enormous variety of high relief designs. It may have derived its name from pre-Christian votive offerings for Wotan since the name, a German diminutive for "Springer," may refer to Wotan's eight-footed charger. During the baroque and rococo periods, cookie molds reached their most elaborate forms in the Germanic parts of Europe and illustrated a great variety of subject matter such as historical events, romantic motifs, portraits, and proverbs as well as religious symbols. These cookies, though edible, were not necessarily made to be eaten; often they portrayed special persons and events and were given as ceremonial gifts.

Today, all cultures make plain and decorative breads that are individually theirs. The challah, a twisted bread in large and small loaves, and the bagel, a hard doughnut-shaped bread, are identified as Jewish breads.

In Sardinia, Italy, a mother will sometimes send her children on their wedding day a basket containing nine loaves of bread with figures of birds and doves outlined in seeds on each one, and another with nine candies of almond paste in the form of doves, hearts, rings, and chains. Four are in pairs to symbolize union.

The Greeks have many symbolic breads. At a person's death a specially decorated 44-pound loaf is eaten as the ceremonial rite of passage, a symbolic act to send the soul of the departed heavenward. Sicilians bake a cookie called "Bones of the Dead" for All Souls' Day, while the same holiday calls for a doll form in Peru. The Mexicans have many symbolic breads for every festival of the year. Wedding breads from Crete, in contrast, are symbols of life and fertility as are those in Italy. Usually baked in the brides' homes, they are often magnificently decorated wreath forms that become an integral part of the wedding ceremony.

Easter time is decorative bread-baking time throughout the Christian world. The Ukrainian bread called "paska" is baked in a round can and decorated with icing and candy. Easter bunnies and lambs are popular with the Germans and Swiss. Polish Easter biscuits are baked in the shape of a farmer's wife with her geese; this represents an appeal to God for good harvests and increasing livestock. There is, in addition, paganism in this association of the resurrection of Christ with the sprouting of planted seeds.

Bread has also appeared in literature. In England there is the johnny boy or Mister London bun (similar to the American gingerbread man), a cookie in the shape of a little boy who comes alive and escapes through the unlatched oven door. German author Wilhelm Busch writes about mischievous children Max and Maurity, the heroes of his stories (on whom the Katzenjammer Kids are based), who fall into the baker's dough in the act of riffling his bread shelf. He puts them in the oven, and they come out in a double bread to escape only by eating their way out.

An unprecedented use of edible bread dough was made by Dorcas Moulton for "The First Artists' Soap Box Derby" in 1975 sponsored by the San Francisco Museum of Art. When Dorcas decided to make her racer of bread, she prevailed upon a commercial bakery to let her use their ovens. The week before the derby, she made molds from heavy foil and cardboard into which she baked 100 pounds of bread using a hot roll mix for the light parts and Russian rye for the dark pieces. The frame was wood and chicken wire with 20-inch bicycle tires covered with bread hubcaps.

This brief history, and any further forays you would want to make into it, should dispel any doubts about bread, edible or inedible, as a medium for artistic creativity.

Bread-dough parties are becoming an exciting event for craft clubs, church groups, and private happenings. Valerie Ann Smith photographed guests of the Great Falls chapter of the Montana Institute of the Arts at work. The party was held in a church kitchen equipped with commercial ovens and adequate counter space; the church was happy to see the facilities used. You can see how engrossed Rex Chamberlain became in his project. (Courtesy, Valerie Ann Smith)

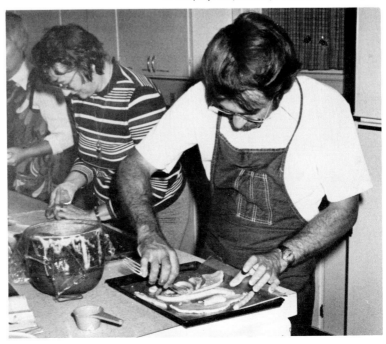

By Rosemary Fee. An antique scale is "weighing" assorted fruit. The clever combination becomes a sculptural object. Fruit is highly glazed with polyurethane varnish.

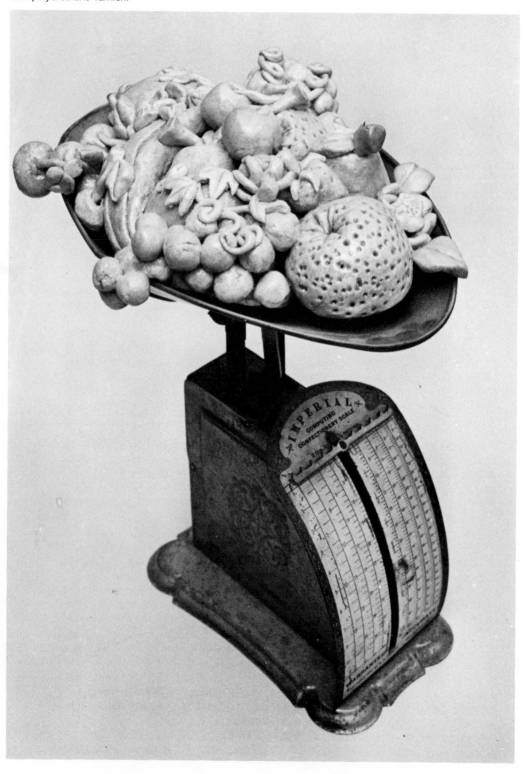

2
BASIC RECIPE NO. 1
-BAKER'S CLAY

The ingredients for making the objects shown throughout this book are as close as your kitchen cabinet. The basic recipe, often called "baker's clay" or "salt dough," consists of flour, salt, and water, mixed and kneaded, then shaped, baked, and sealed. What could be less expensive and more easily available for an expressive art medium?

Once mixed, the dough has a satiny texture, a delicious aroma; it begs to be touched and rolled between the fingers, manipulated with the hands. Do not be surprised if everyone in the family begins to pick up pieces and work them into forms. Do not be shocked, either, if you find yourself in the kitchen all day, and there is nothing to eat for dinner. Creating with dough can become such an addiction that you will not notice how quickly time passes.

The procedure for working with baker's clay is:

A. *Mix the Ingredients* and knead until very smooth, about five to ten minutes.
B. *Create the Object:* Several methods for shaping the dough into art forms are illustrated in the following chapters.
C. *Bake* until rock hard and thoroughly dry. Before and during the baking process some precoloring and glazing can be done.
D. *Finish* by surface coloring and sealing. Sealing with varnish prevents moisture from reentering the dough, which causes mold or deterioration.

There is no one way to work with bread dough. Artists who shared their working methods consistently contradicted one another's findings, yet all their methods work. During interviews, the following was revealed:

"A gas oven is better than electric." "An electric oven is better than gas."

"Objects brown more evenly at low temperatures." "Objects brown more evenly at high temperatures."

A Teflon cookie sheet is better; the artwork bakes faster." "An aluminum cookie sheet is best."

Objects should be put in the oven as soon as they are made." "Objects can be left to air dry and form a light crust; it gives a nicer texture."

All of which shows that anything goes. The same is true for supplies. What you do not have, improvise. For instance, no cookie sheet? Use the bottom of a cake pan turned upside down. No rolling pin? Use the side of a glass or jar.

How durable are finished bread-dough pieces? They can last for years provided they are thoroughly baked and properly sealed. Kay Whitcomb has pieces in which the wire hanger rusted after years, but the sculpture is still perfect. Bread dough is more durable than ceramics; most will not break when dropped (except for small protuberances). Generally, bread-dough objects should not be used in bathrooms or any place where they will be subjected to excessive moisture.

Use this chapter as a basic reference for materials and procedures, then pick up nuggets of additional working information in the following chapters.

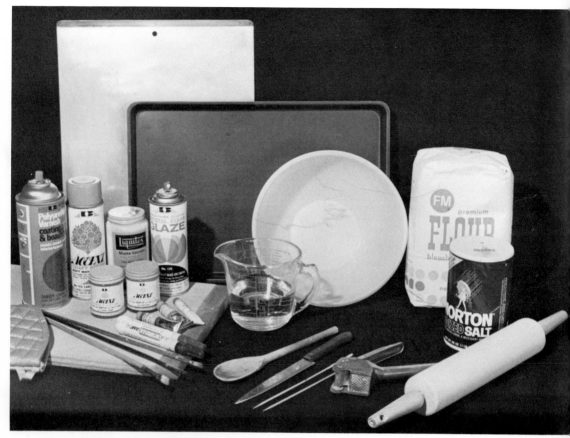

Basic supplies include flour, salt, water, measuring cup, mixing bowl and spoon, heavy-duty cookie sheets, wood skewers or toothpicks, cutting instruments, a garlic press, rolling pin, colorants, sealers, and brushes.

A. MIXING AND KNEADING

There are many variations of this recipe, but the most often used is:

4 cups flour
1 cup salt
1½ cups water

Mixing Method A: Mix salt in warm water until partially dissolved, then add to flour.

Mixing Method B: Mix flour and salt, then add water.

With both methods, mix with a spoon until the particles stick together, then form into a ball with your hands and begin to knead.

The two mixing methods are given because of different consistencies of flours. Some knead up more quickly with one method than another, and it is up to you to experiment. Generally, use the cheapest flour you can buy. Because of bleaches and preservatives added to various brands of flour, some will yield different textures and may vary in color from very white to slightly yellow. Dark flours such as whole wheat, rye, pumpernickel, and buckwheat are used the same way. Old flour you may no longer trust for food can be used. Use the cheapest brand of salt you can find; it does not matter whether it is plain or iodized.

Kneading means to press the dough into a form or mass with your hands; the longer you knead the dough, the smoother it becomes. Knead the dough

16

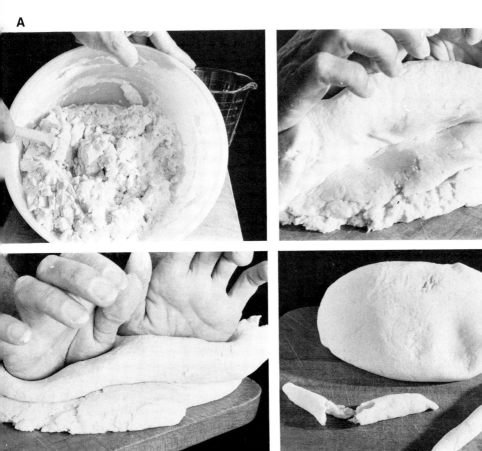

A. Mix ingredients until they begin to congeal. Use your hands to finish gathering all the dough into a ball.

C. Knead by folding dough in half and pushing with heels of hands. Fold in corners, push, repeat until a texture that resembles baby's skin results. Knead at least 5 minutes, often more.

B. Remove from bowl and begin to knead on a hard, flat surface; flour the surface lightly if dough sticks. Dough is still highly textured and rough after about 2 minutes.

D. When dough is smooth, it is ready for use. If a rolled coil splits *(left)*, dough needs more kneading until the coil holds together *(right)*.

until satiny smooth; it will take five to ten minutes, sometimes more, depending upon the consistency of the dough and how smooth you want your finished objects to appear.

Knead by flattening the ball of dough, then folding and pushing it with the heels of your hands, fold in the corners, the front, the back, and keep working it until it has the texture of baby's skin. If the dough does not knead up properly and remains highly textured and crumbly, add a few drops of water at a time and work until it becomes satiny smooth. If it becomes too moist and sticky, add flour. The dough is ideal when it is stiff rather than mushy and moist.

Dough that is not sufficiently kneaded will be difficult to form and may fall apart during baking. It will retain cracks and result in an uneven surface. Dough that is too moist will rise and puff up during baking.

Mixed dough dries out quickly when it is exposed to air. Keep the ball of dough in a plastic bag or covered bowl and take out only what you need as you work. For smaller projects, mix only half a recipe. It is best to use up dough in about four hours. Unused dough can be stored in a plastic container in the refrigerator for days, sometimes weeks, and then used. Usually, stored refrigerated dough becomes moist and sticky and requires the addition of flour to bring it back to working consistency. If in doubt, discard and mix a new batch. Sometimes your best creative efforts will happen when you are using old dough; and if it does not bake properly, you will hate yourself later.

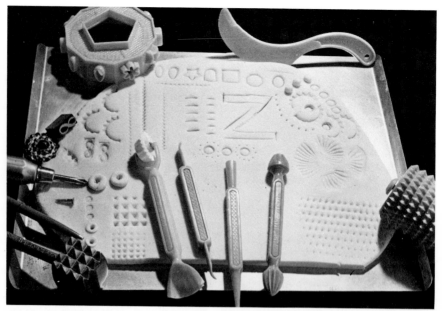

A variety of implements (improvised from objects in your kitchen drawer and toolbox) is used for texturing, cutting, making designs and shapes. Plastic tools made especially for working with bread dough are inexpensive and an excellent investment. Tools shown and the designs they make are (clockwise) metal meat tenderizer, ball-point pen point and cap, screwhead, Phillips screwdriver, buttons, print type, and the assorted "Natcol" shapers: banana cutting knife and design implements. Object (right) is a plastic meat tenderizer.

B. CREATING THE OBJECT

Once you decide what you want to create, the next decision is how to make it. Each of the following chapters discusses approaches and working methods. No matter which methods you use and how inventively you combine them, all require basic procedures. Use this list as a working guide and as a check for any questions that may arise.

All dough parts must be joined with water. Water acts as the glue medium. If parts are not joined properly, the dough may separate during baking and split when cooled. Water should be applied with a brush or dabbed on with the fingers . . . always very sparingly.

Adhere thin pieces of dough by pushing an instrument through them in addition to moistening to make a functional and decorative seal. Use the eraser end of a pencil, the retracted point of a ball-point pen, a toothpick, screwdriver, or plastic bread-dough tool.

Shape the objects directly on a baking sheet or on a piece of aluminum foil on a baking sheet. Baking sheets may be Teflon or aluminum. They should be heavy duty because thin sheets tend to warp during baking and cause the object on it to warp also.

Impressing can be done with a variety of objects and is used in almost all decorating procedures. Impressions hold up best with stiffer dough. If dough is too moist and soft, dust area with flour and then make the impression.

Cut straight edges with a sharp knife or the plastic banana-shape dough tool. Knives often leave ragged edges that can give a nice texture; the banana tool cuts a smooth edge. Also, cut with pizza cutters, carrot slicers, and so on for decorative edges. Ragged edges can be smoothed by moistening the finger with water and rubbing.

Small objects can be baked solid; large pieces can be molded over shapes of aluminum foil (see chapter 4) so that they bake through and thoroughly. Very small objects can be placed on toothpicks and baked upright stuck into sand or salt in a bakeproof dish.

Analyze a form you want to make and decide if it should be done as one piece, as two pieces baked separately and glued together, or as two pieces made by the double-bake method (see chapter 5).

Always remember to add hanging devices into backs of pieces *before* baking if they are to be hung. Use Christmas ornament hooks, pieces of bent wire, circles from pop-top drink cans, or halves of paper clips pushed into the dough at top center, close to the back of the piece. If you forget, glue a long doubled length of nylon fishing line all along the back of the figure from top to bottom, leaving the loop extending at the top. Cover with masking tape. You can use a wood drill bit to poke a hole in the back for placing on a hook if you prefer.

Large objects should be strengthened with wire. (See demonstration by Kay Whitcomb on page 51.) Dough itself has no strength and requires armatures for connecting and supporting. Where dough connects in small pieces, it is often wise to add toothpicks or wires between parts such as head and neck, arms and legs to body. When a piece is hung from the top, lack of connecting supports can result in the bottom portions separating from the top in time.

Hair, fringe, and similar effects are created by pushing the dough through a garlic press (see pages 53 and 97). Lengths of cooked spaghetti can also be added onto or around the object. Raw noodles or pasta in any shape can be placed on the dough and baked.

Make or buy miniature accessories. Combine items made with Recipe No. 2 (chapter 3) and bake in or add on by gluing. Heavy or thick plastic items, sequins, and metallic fabrics can be baked into the dough at low temperatures. Thin plastics will melt. Always pretest meltability by placing a sample on a square of dough and baking it for an hour.

Always grease forms over which dough will be molded so the baked dough will separate from the form. Use smooth forms with no undercuts.

Use branches, twigs, pods, acorns, seeds, shells, peppercorns, corianders, cloves, and poppyseeds along with your dough art. Any found objects from the outdoors should be baked in the oven for about an hour at about 250° to kill off any tiny inhabitants that may be lurking within.

Breaks and cracks in baked pieces can be repaired with white glue or a household cement and by mixing white glue with sanded particles of dough and forcing into the crack. Fresh dough can be added between broken pieces, in a crack or broken air bubble and rebaked, then sanded or camouflaged with gesso or the paint and sealer.

If an object softens after some time, rebake and reseal.

THE DOUGH IS INEDIBLE . . . DO *NOT* EAT IT.

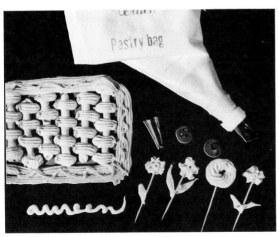

Cake-decorating tubes with large nozzles can be used for making myriad designs. Ideas can be gleaned from cake-decorating books. Dough must be used soft with extra water added. It may be blended in an electric mixer.

Basic forming techniques are used in this clown by Marian Gault: circles, coils, rolled portions, impressing, pinching, and "hair" made with a garlic press. *(Photo, Ned Gault)*

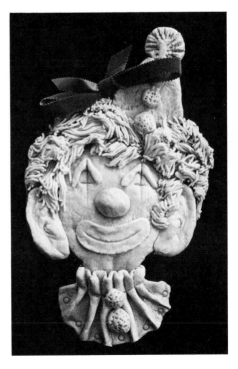

C. BAKING

Bread-dough objects must be baked until they are thoroughly dried and almost rock hard. Optimum baking temperatures are between 275° and 325° for about ½ hour per ¼-inch thickness of dough. Begin with these temperatures and then experiment. Generally, higher temperatures will brown the dough faster. At lower temperatures the dough will remain whiter. It is not unusual to bake pieces overnight; sometimes for days.

Most people place objects in the oven as soon as possible, but sometimes pieces may be air dried in a warm room or out in the sun, then baked for shorter periods of time than those that you pop in the oven immediately. Air-dried pieces may have tiny surface cracks that can be covered by painting. These can result in a preferred surface texture.

Pieces composed of thin and thick parts will brown at different rates, and the thin portions may begin to burn before the thick parts are finished. Cover the browned parts with a piece of aluminum foil to prevent further browning.

When a large object is hard enough to remove from the pan, it may be turned over so the heat penetrates the bottom thoroughly. When hard, it can be placed directly on the rack. Objects baked over forms, such as bread baskets and sculptures, should be released from the form when hard. Continue baking until dry throughout. Bread dough contracts as it cools; to prevent breaking, remove objects from forms before cooling.

Air bubbles trapped in the dough may result in unwanted puffy areas during baking. Watch the objects, especially during the first hour; if bubbles appear, lower the oven temperature, poke the puffs with a toothpick or pin, then place a metal knife handle, brick, or ovenproof bowl on the object to flatten. Objects should be weighted only *after* they have formed a hard outer crust so the weight does not dent the surface design.

Thin, flat pieces that tend to warp during baking should be weighted also. If they do not straighten out, redampen by placing the object in the bathroom while taking a shower. When soft enough, flatten gently, weight, rebake, and seal immediately.

Always use potholders to shift pans in the oven and to remove objects. It is easy to become enthusiastic about the little forms you are baking and pick them up without thinking. Cool on a rack as you would any baked foods.

Backs of objects can be signed with a waterproof felt-tip marker or pen and ink, then brushed with a sealing coat before cooling (see Finishing). After acrylics and other water-base paints are used for surface coloring, the piece should be returned to the oven for about ten minutes of baking to dry out any moisture it may have absorbed from the paint.

If an object has been stored for some time before sealing, it is wise to rebake for about half an hour and then finish. Much depends on your climate. Artists who live near water have more problems with moisture than those who live in dry, desert climates. If you sell your objects to a wide audience, sealing techniques must be impeccable as you never know where the object will be placed.

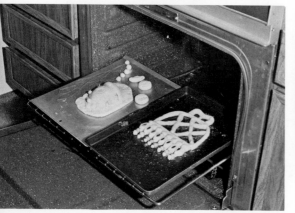

Baking can be done on a cookie sheet in any home oven. After objects harden, they may be removed from sheet and placed on the rack.

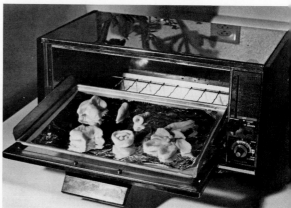

A small baking appliance set at the proper temperature is convenient for small objects.

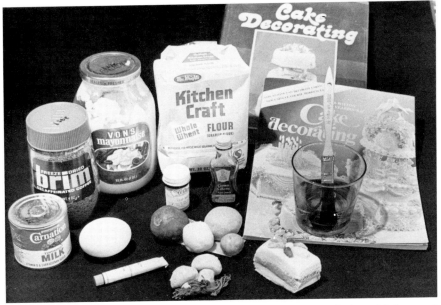

Raw dough may be colored with paste and liquid food coloring and water-base paints. Several food items can be applied during baking to yield different shades of beiges and browns. Colored flours can be substituted for white flour.

Precoloring and Glazing

Some coloring may be added to the dough before and during baking to minimize or eliminate hand painting after the object is baked. Use different flour recipes, such as whole wheat and rye, in combination with white-flour recipe for easy precoloring.

Before Baking—Raw dough can be precolored by adding drops of liquid or paste food coloring, tube watercolors, colored inks, and fabric dyes. Powdered colorants such as dyes should be mixed with the flour and salt before adding water. Different strengths of diluted instant coffee can be used as a portion of the water originally mixed with the dough. After the dough is kneaded, additions can be tube watercolors, liquid and paste food coloring.

Food coloring is efficient because it enables you to mix up small batches of different colored doughs quickly. Add the coloring by placing a few drops of liquid or a fingerful of paste on a piece of dough, then kneading it in thoroughly. Paste coloring is vivid; liquid is more pastel.

During Baking—Many unique glazes have been suggested for coloring and glazing the dough while it is being baked. These should be added before and/or any time during the baking. The more applications of the glaze during the baking period, the darker it usually becomes. Glazes can be added to the entire piece or to different portions in varying amounts to result in many tones on one piece. Glazes should be brushed on with soft bristle paintbrushes for small pieces, wider brushes for large areas. Try the following and conduct your own experiments.

● Egg. Beat the egg with a fork, and add one tablespoon of water. One or more coats will yield different shades from beige to a leathery brown. Try the yolk alone mixed with water. Try the white alone mixed with water. For simultaneous color and glaze, dilute the egg, whole or separated, to brushing consistency with colors of acrylic paint and water. Or add a few drops of food coloring to the egg-water mix and paint on.

● Mayonnaise. Same procedure as above.

● Condensed Milk. Sometimes yields a marbleized or a splotchy effect. Add spices such as curry, cinnamon, or turmeric for color and a pleasant odor.

● Instant Coffee. Add two tablespoons to egg or condensed milk for a brown glaze.

● Water. Brush on a thin coat overall before baking.

● Liquid Shoe Polish and Colored Leather Dyes. Rub or brush on lightly after the first 15 minutes of baking.

Oven temperatures will affect the brownness of the piece with and without glazes. Highest temperatures increase brownness.

D. FINISHING

Many people prefer the natural look of the baked bread dough for the final color, while others feel that painted color is essential. Both practices require certain finishing procedures and final sealing coats to keep out moisture.

Surface Colorants

A variety of coloring material can be applied to the finished, cooled bread-dough item. Generally, water-base paints are preferred to oil base. No matter what colorants you use, any time you add unlike coloring layers over one another, it is good practice to use a coat of sealer between them to prevent any color from running, smearing, dulling, and bubbling. For example, if you have used watercolors and then feel you would like the deeper tones of acrylics, apply a spray coat of craft sealer over the watercolor first or the moisture in the acrylic can cause incompatibility problems. Buy sealers such as IB Seal N Fix, those sold for decoupage or other crafts and for fixatives for artists' paints. Always pretest paint compatibility on a scrap piece of dough, then mark the paints used and the results on the scrap piece so you will have a record for future testing.

The following surface colorants are all applicable:

acrylic paint colors	pen and ink	antiquing glazes
watercolors	fabric dyes	varnish stains
felt-tip markers	vegetable coloring	decoupage paints
gouache	colored pencils	assorted metallic finishes
waterproof casein	tempera or poster paints	gesso

Acrylic paints are the most popular and efficient coloring, available in jars in brushing consistency, in spray cans, and in tubes that can be mixed with water. They mix easily and dry quickly. Mix acrylic tube coloring in small quantities in plastic ice-cube trays; cover the tray with a plastic bag when you are finished. Next time you can add water to the acrylics again, and they are ready for use, thus eliminating waste.

You can achieve a ceramiclike appearance with bread dough by applying a coat of gesso, a white plasterlike, thick substance, for a ground, then painting over the gesso. Gesso also fills in cracks and holes. Pieces coated with gesso completely camouflage the nature of the material and can be made to resemble fine china or ceramics with the convenience of bread dough as a medium. You can achieve a porcelainlike finish by brushing two or three layers of white glue over a brightly painted surface, drying thoroughly between coats. Brush slowly to avoid bubbles. Wet glue will appear cloudy, but it dries to a clear glaze. When dry, finish with a high gloss varnish.

Unusual finishes can be attained by adding antiquing glaze over a painted or stained coat that has been sealed—the sealer provides a smooth surface

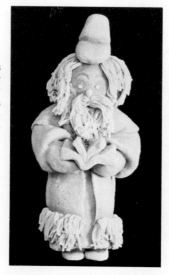
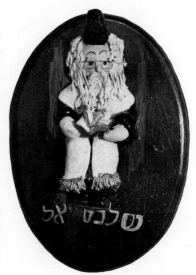

A Rabbi. By Grace Kramer (Gracie's Creations). A figure taken directly from the oven is light beige. After painting and sealing, the figure is mounted on a varnished plaque. Eyeglasses are formed with thin gold wire and glued in place.

22

for the glaze and rub-on finishes to slide over so you can achieve different effects. Try brass, gold, pewter, and also flourescent paints that will glow under black light.

For facial features use cosmetics. Seal them before adding other paints.

Paintbrushes

Paintbrushes are important tools. Use fine brushes for hand painting and broad brushes for applying sealers. For some details you can use disposable cotton tips and pipe cleaners. Always clean brushes thoroughly after using and dry with the bristles up. Brushes used with acrylics must be kept in water; if they dry hard, they must be soaked in a special acrylic solvent. Brushes used for varnishes should be cleaned with turpentine or paint thinner.

SEALING

The importance of sealing bread-dough objects to prevent moisture from reentering and causing mold has already been emphasized. You have a wide choice of final coatings, and you may want to experiment with them for appearance and durability in your climate. A final sealer must be transparent and nonpenetrating so it fortifies the surface with a hard protective coating. The best choice is a polyurethane varnish that can be brushed or sprayed on over the natural or painted bread-dough object. Varnishes without a urethane base (those that were used until the synthetic products were introduced) usually are harder to apply and require long drying times.

Varnishes are available in matte, satin, and high gloss finishes. Polyurethane casting resins may be used for dipping pieces into when a thick, glass-like coating is desired. You can also brush on certain resins such as those used for boat hulls and coating surfboards. They are referred to as surfacing or polyester laminating resin. These require the addition of a catalyst.

Lacquer is also a satisfactory, fast-drying, transparent finish but not as durable as varnish. Shellac is not recommended as it is incompatible with many of the sealers and varnishes. Clear white glue and acrylic medium can be applied to the backs of warm bread-dough pieces for a good sealer that will penetrate crevices that close up after cooling; this is added interior protection against moisture.

All varnishes should be applied with a minimum of four coats; some people use as many as nine. It is best to apply several thin layers of varnish in preference to one or two heavily applied layers that may sag or bubble.

Spray painting should be done out-of-doors, if possible, or in a well-ventilated room. Place the object in an open box to confine the spray. For hand and spray painting, a small turntable such as those sold for organizing kitchen cabinets is convenient. Cover it with wax paper or foil for easy cleanup and to avoid paper adhering to the object.

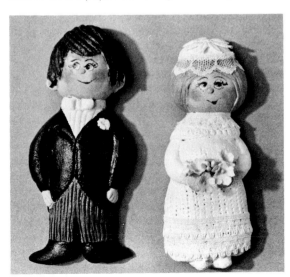

By Virginia Black. A bride and groom finished with acrylic paints and a matte varnish. The bride's skirt and hat are actual pieces of lace glued over the dough figure and sealed. Eyes, lips, hair, and flowers are hand painted with acrylics; cheeks are cosmetic rouge.

23

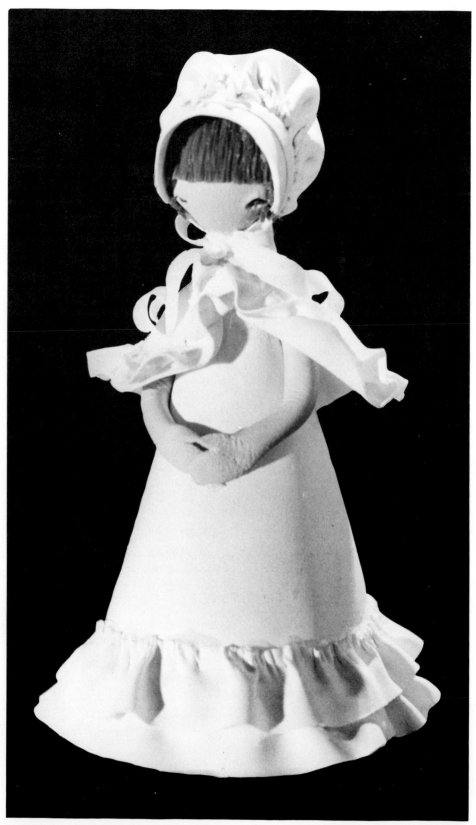

By Linda Fugate. This delicate, beautifully crafted figure made over a toothpick is only 2½″
high, about ⅓ the size it is actually shown. For
display purposes it is placed under a glass
dome.

3
RECIPE NO. 2 −BREAD AND GLUE

Recipe No. 2 is a no-bake mixture that is particularly adaptable to small delicate forms. It can be used by itself or in conjunction with Recipe No. 1, Baker's Clay. The essential ingredients—slices of white bread and glue, mixed with a softener such as liquid detergent or glycerin—result in a pliable mixture that can be rolled paper thin so that miniature objects can be created. It is the recipe used by Ecuadorians for their traditional figures. The Mexicans call it "migajón" and fashion it into flowered jewelry that resembles fine china. People who decorate eggs find it indispensable for miniature interior environments.

The recipe and mixing procedure that follow result in a batch of dough about the size of the palm of your hand. But that small blob can go a long way as you will observe once you begin working with it.

The advantage of this recipe is that you get exactly the shape you design as there is no baking involved: The objects air dry and are sealed with a brushed-on mixture of equal parts of white glue and water. A minimum of three coats of sealer should be used (allowed to dry between coats). Varnishes, craft glazes, and clear nail polish are also recommended. Sealing prevents the pieces from drying out, cracking, and becoming moldy. A sealed object may be baked at 350° for three to five minutes for a high gloss.

Dough should be stored in plastic bags within plastic refrigerator storage containers to keep it fresh and prevent mold. It can last for weeks.

As you work, pinch off small bits of the dough, keeping the excess within a plastic bag. If the dough tends to dry out, add in a little more glue and reknead. When you take a batch from the refrigerator, work it in your hands until it warms up and is pliable.

To attach parts to one another, use dabs of glue. For adhering heavy pieces, use Duco or other household cement.

Work small pieces on toothpicks or wires, and then place the bottom ends in a piece of plastic foam or clay so the objects dry. Larger pieces can be worked on long wood skewers or on drink-mixing sticks: These provide an armature and a handle by which to hold and turn the object as you paint it.

Place flat objects on wax paper to dry so they will not stick. Drying takes about twelve hours or longer, depending on thickness. Check the objects as they dry as some changes can be made when the pieces are still in a semi-plastic state.

Dough can be colored by mixing in paste or liquid food colors, tube watercolors, or liquid temperas. Acrylics dry too fast and make the dough dry out. Pinch off pieces of the dough and knead in different colors. Simply add a dab of the colorant onto the dough, fold it in, and knead until the dough is evenly colored throughout. By partially kneading, you can get a marbleized effect.

Always clean and dry scissors and other tools immediately to prevent rust.

With the exception of the recipe and drying techniques, the majority of procedures described for Recipe No. 1 are applicable to Recipe No. 2; both mixtures are adaptable to sculptural form: impressing and embedding, rolling, building up shapes with balls and coils. The painting procedures, too, are the same.

Among the nice features of this recipe is that you can take the dough out of the refrigerator and work at odd moments. You need only a small working space so that you can be creative even if you live in a camper or a tiny apartment.

THE RECIPE

Use any kind of day-old white bread—regular, French, sourdough—with the crusts cut away.

- 3 slices white bread (not sandwich sliced)
- 3 tablespoons white glue (the cheapest you can find)

Optional Ingredients:

- 1 teaspoon white shoe polish (or acrylic paint)
- 1 teaspoon glycerin from the drugstore (or ½ teaspoon liquid detergent)
- 3 drops lemon juice

At least one of the optional ingredients should be added, or all of them. Shoe polish and acrylic paint add whiteness to the dough. Glycerin, detergent, and lemon juice soften the dough and prevent it from cracking and bubbling. Double all the ingredients to double the recipe.

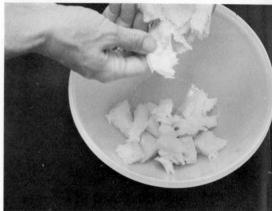

Remove crusts and tear bread into small pieces. Mix ingredients together until the mixture no longer sticks to your fingers and has a smooth texture. Kneading may take 6 to 10 minutes. If it adheres to your hand, rub a few drops of glycerin or other hand lotion on your hands.

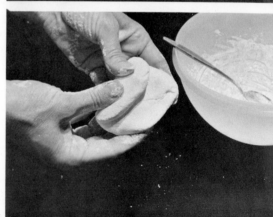

After about 10 minutes of kneading, the sticky quality will disappear, and the ingredients will rub off your hands and congeal into a smooth, soft ball of dough. Place in plastic bag.

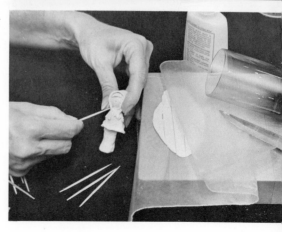

Thin layers of dough are rolled with a glass or rolling pin between layers of waxed paper. For a figure, begin by placing a rolled oval for the head onto a toothpick, then cutting patterns as you would for clothing and draping it around, modeling and designing the form as you go with any instrument that will work—toothpicks, pins, darning needles. Cut away excess areas with manicure scissors or a very sharp knife.

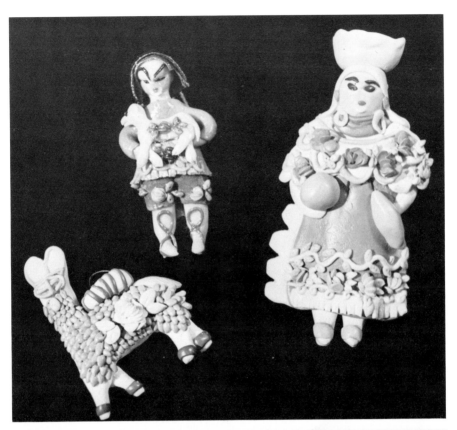

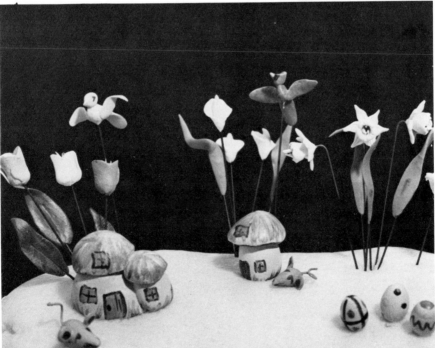

Above: A 3¼″ high Ecuadorian bread-dough figure has been reinterpreted in a modern mood by Bernice A. Houston. The llama is 3″ high; the girl is 5″ high.

Below: Yvonne Righter creates mini-miniatures, each delicately formed on a wire stem. The flowers and birds are ⁵⁄₁₆″ high. The small mouse is ³⁄₈″ long; his house ⁵⁄₈″ high.

FLOWERS
How to Make a Rose

Bernice A. Houston demonstrates how to make a rose (see color section) and bridal basket, detail on opposite page. You will need the prepared dough, lengths of #26 gauge floral wire, floral tape, white glue, real leaves (for impressing the design in the dough), acrylic finish, and manicure or surgical scissors.

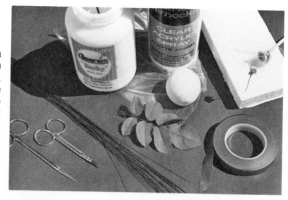

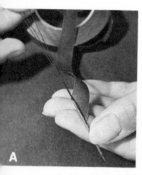
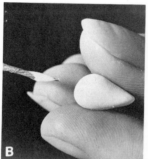
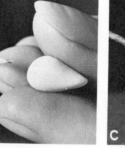
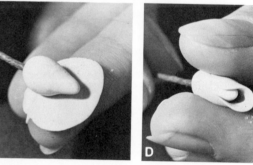

A. Use three lengths of wire for the stem. Lay the tape on the wire on an angle, and twist the wires as you work the tape down and around them.

B. Roll a small piece of dough into a ball and then reshape into a teardrop and place on the stem end that has been dipped in glue.

C. Flatten a small piece of dough and wrap it around the rose center to begin a buildup of petals.

D. The petal is shaped, the ends overlapped and secured with a dab of white glue. Each petal end, in turn, should be secured with a dab of glue.

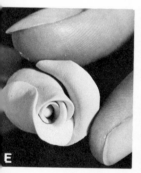
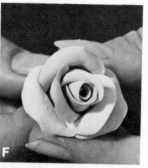
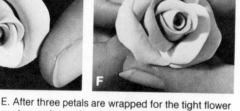
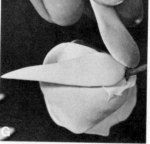
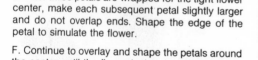
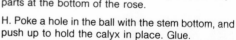

E. After three petals are wrapped for the tight flower center, make each subsequent petal slightly larger and do not overlap ends. Shape the edge of the petal to simulate the flower.

F. Continue to overlay and shape the petals around the center until the flower is the size you want.

G. The calyx (made of green-colored dough) consists of five teardrop-shaped flat pieces held by a ball of dough. Use a dab of glue to place the calyx parts at the bottom of the rose.

H. Poke a hole in the ball with the stem bottom, and push up to hold the calyx in place. Glue.

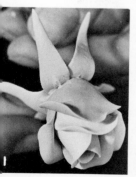
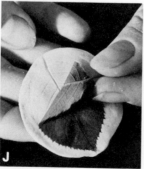
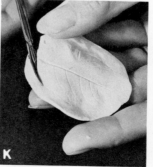
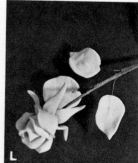

I. Bend the calyx parts downward.

J. Leaves are made by impressing a real leaf against a shape of dough. Press hard so the veining is impressed. Remove the leaf.

K. Cut around the outline with a manicure scissors.

L. Three finished leaves. Each is placed on a stem made of two wrapped wires so it is thinner than the main stem. Leaf ends are bent along the main stem and wrapped with tape.

How to Make Lilies of the Valley

Lily-of-the-valley sprigs are made by pressing a small circle of dough on the end of a rounded wood dough tool tip, gluing in stamen made by rolling bits of dough between your fingers and then gluing them along a wrapped wire stem. (See Bouquet, below, and page 30.) For additional flower shapes refer to seed catalogs and cake-decorating books. Pull real flowers apart to analyze how they are made and then emulate them in dough.

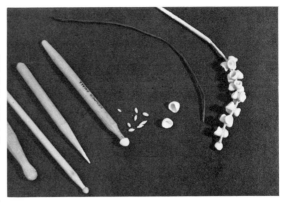

Below: Flower Girl's Bouquet. By Bernice A. Houston. Flowers formed on wires and toothpicks are set into a plastic-foam base within a woven basket. The roses, stephanotis, and lilies of the valley are combined with tulle and ribbon.

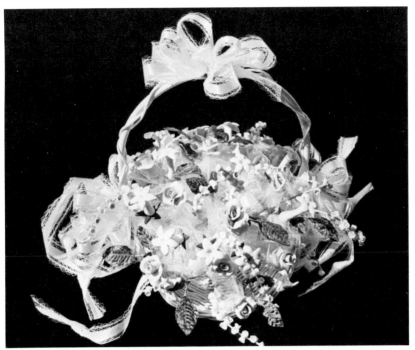

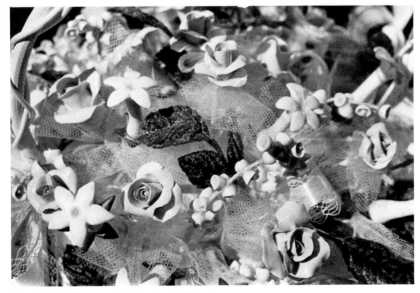

Detail, Bridal Bouquet. By Bernice A. Houston.

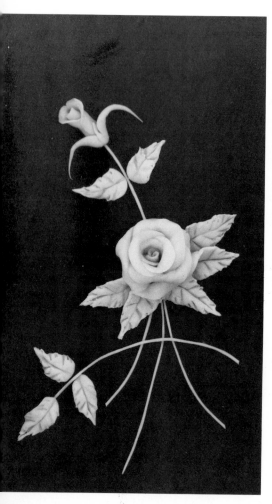

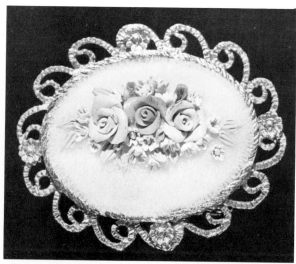

Above: Brooch. By Bernice A. Houston. White velvet ribbon and tiny bread-dough flowers are glued onto an oval cut from a plastic coffee-can lid and placed in a jewelry finding.

Left: Rose and bud mounted on black velvet and framed. By Ruth Dawson Barry. *(Courtesy, Savage's Trading Post, El Portal, California)*

MINIATURES

A variety of figures can be made by reducing shapes to circles and ovals and combining them using dabs of glue as the medium to hold parts together.

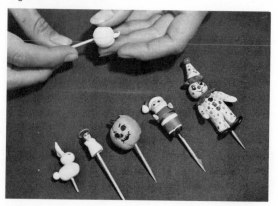

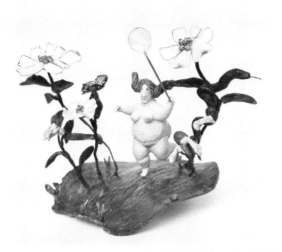

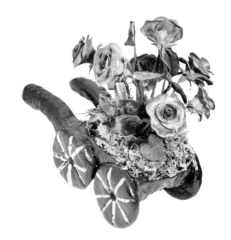

Above: Wood Nymph. By Linda Talaba. About 7″ high. *(Courtesy, artist)*

Above right: Wheelbarrows made of baker's clay with flowers made of the bread and glue recipe. Left object is 5″ high. By Lotte Hunt and Judy Burbridge. Right piece is 3″ high, 4″ wide. By Lotte Hunt.

Below: Old Mother Goose and her transportation. By Chomy Garces of Fantasy Creations.

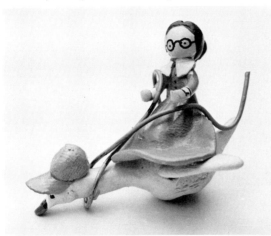

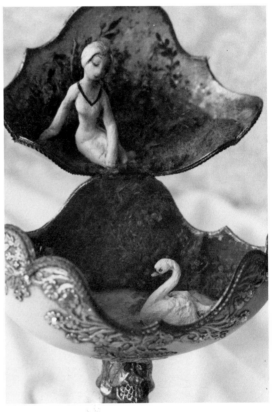

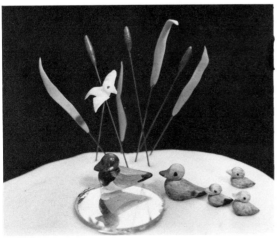

Above: A delicately formed maiden and a swan made of dough are placed within a jeweled and richly designed egg. By Sally LeVan. *(Courtesy, artist)*

Left: A duck family by Yvonne Righter. Sizes range from 5/16″ long to 5/8″ long. They are perfect for egg decorating and making miniatures.

31

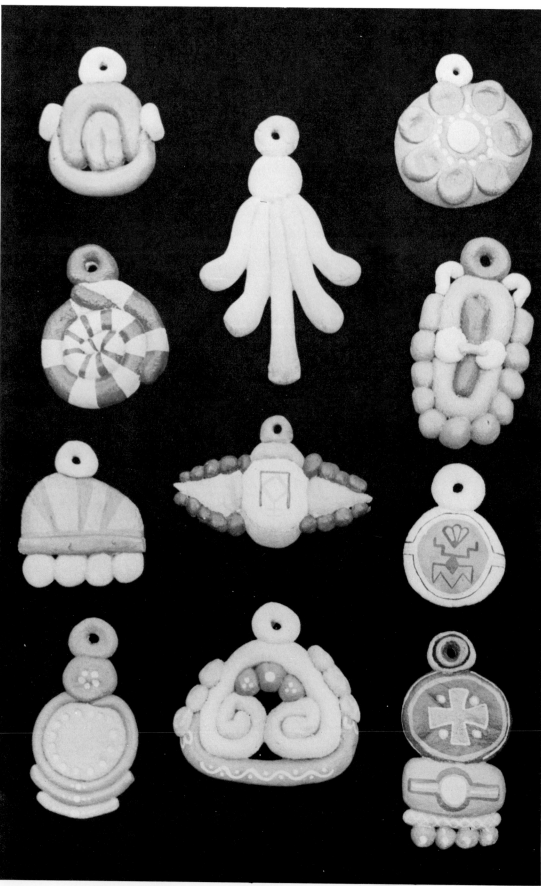

Ornaments for hanging or wearing. By Shannon
Yewell. The use of the simple ball and coil in infinite
arrangements is a basic design element for bread-
dough creations.

4
WORKING METHODS –THE BALL AND THE COIL

Once a batch of dough is mixed, the inevitable temptation is to pinch off a piece and begin rolling it between your hands and think, "What shall I make?" That small ball of dough is to bread-dough art almost what the atom is to matter. You can poke into it and form a face, roll it into a coil, punch it and make a doughnut shape, add more balls to it and begin to develop form and design. The possibilities are infinite and limited only by your imagination.

All the objects shown in this chapter begin with a rolled ball or coil and graduate to other basic geometric shapes placed next to or on top of one another. The painter Paul Cézanne observed that "everything in nature can be reduced to cylinders, cones and spheres," and that certainly holds true when forming bread-dough pieces. After you learn to analyze objects and reduce them to basic shapes, it will be easy to create them with dough.

Where do you get ideas for bread-dough figures? Observe them in art books, current fashion magazines, doll-making books, and costume books. Hair styles can be gleaned from the same sources. Assorted, artistically rendered children and animal ideas can be discovered in juvenile books.

If drawing eyes and other features looms as an obstacle, notice how lines needed can be simply made; for eyes, use two parallel ovals for an upper lid, a semicircle for the bottom, and a dot for the pupil. Try to stylize features rather than make them real. Study the eyes and mouths drawn in the figures by Virginia Black and see how simple they are. Place coriander seeds where eyesockets are, and you will not have to worry about drawing them.

Animals, too, can be reduced to a series of circles, ovals, and coils to make them whimsical and cute. Do not try for a photographic rendition; rather strive for a gesture, a feeling, a way of expressing your interpretation of the real being.

Want to make objects from nature? Then glean ideas from encyclopedias, seashell books, scientific magazines, *National Geographic* illustrations, and similar sources.

Ideas for trimming and decorating figures will come from your imagination and the tools you work with. Refer also to cookbooks, cake-decorating books, and design books.

All the sources mentioned can help you with coloring ideas, too. If you are hesitant about which colors go well together, use a color wheel (in an encyclopedia under "Color") and experiment with the primary colors—yellow, red, and blue—to learn how they mix to form secondary and tertiary colors. Books on acrylic and watercolor painting will give you all the information you need about mixing colors.

Combine your bread-dough figures with real objects such as shells, seedpods, twigs, pebbles, yarn, sequins, glitter, ribbon, lace, some baked, others glued on afterward.

In all your bread-dough efforts attempt originality rather than copying exactly the objects shown. You can emulate them for technique, but strike out on your own so you can be truly creative and design pieces that are individually and uniquely yours.

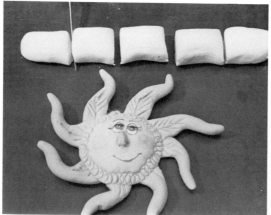

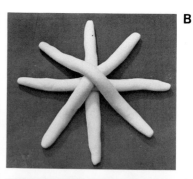

CREATE A SUNBURST WITH COILS AND CIRCLES

Virginia Black demonstrates the procedure for making an elegant sunburst with coils and circles. Remember that touching portions of dough must be moistened with water slightly so they adhere. Insert wire for hanging before baking.

A. Begin with a ball of dough that will fit easily in the palm of your hand. Roll into a coil, and cut into five even pieces. Four will be used for the sun's rays.

B. Roll each of the four pieces into a coil about 5" long. Overlay, as shown.

C. Twist the ends with your fingers.

D. Flatten the center with the heel of your hand.

E. Roll the fifth piece into a ball and flatten. Moisten the center to receive the flattened circle for the sun's face.

F. Impress an overlap circle design around the edge with the open cover of a ball-point pen or other round instrument.

G. Roll a small ball for the nose, and reshape into a teardrop. Apply in center of sun's face. Eyes and mouth can be impressed also or painted on. Bake about 1½ hours (or until rock hard) in 300° oven. Paint as desired, and seal with minimum of three coats of matte or gloss varnish.

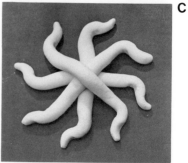

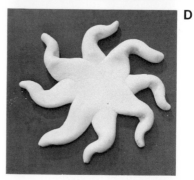

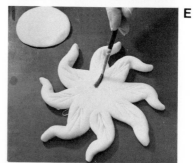

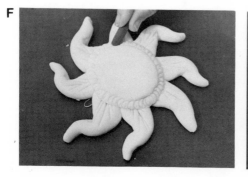

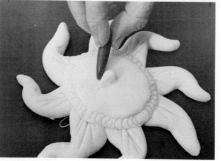

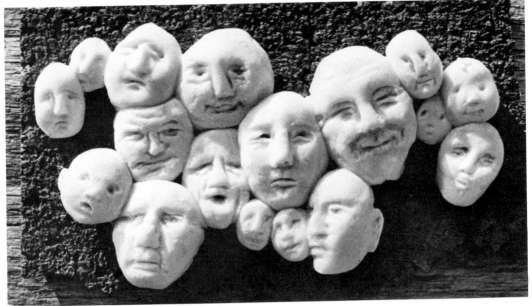

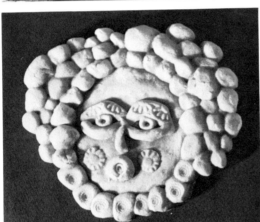

Above: Heads by Lois Crachy are shaped from different size balls of dough formed into ovals for heads with a variety of expressions. They are natural color mounted on dark cork, which is placed on a rectangle of gray weathered wood for contrast and "frame."

Left: By Mimi Levinson. A caricature of one of her children accomplished with circles and coils.

Below left: Another version of a sunburst. By Marian Gault. *(Photo, Ned Gault)*

Below: By Kathie Fujisaka. Coils and circles are cleverly shaped to become a little lamb. *(Courtesy, artist)*

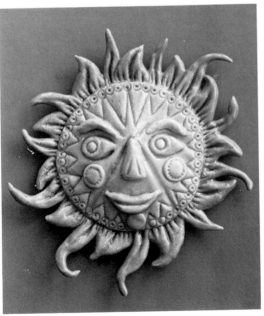

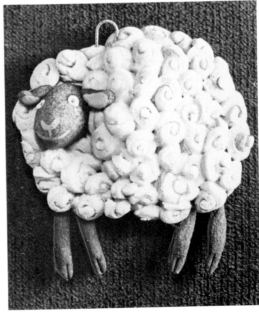

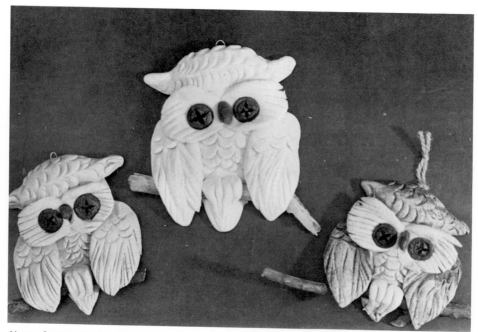

Above: Owls by Virginia Black are made from the nine shaped pieces of dough shown at right. Eyes are embedded seedpods from a tree; the nose is a pebble. She shows how to create it:

CREATE AN OWL WITH OVALS AND CIRCLES

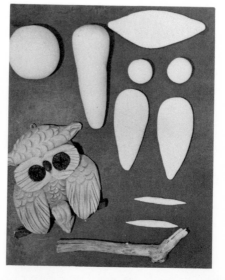

A. The twig is placed across the bottom of the body. The two thin coils are curved in half and shaped into feet that grasp the twig.

B. The body feathers are made by gently cutting scallops into and lifting pieces of the dough with the end of a narrow glass pill bottle.

C. Water is brushed along the sides of the body to receive wings.

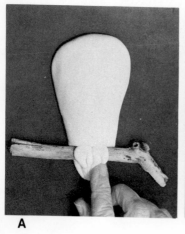

A

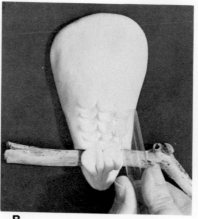

B

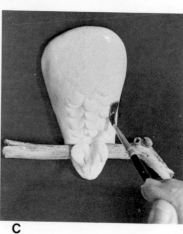

C

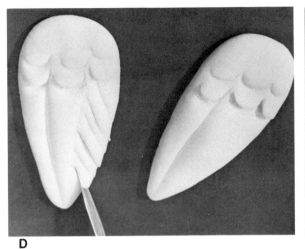

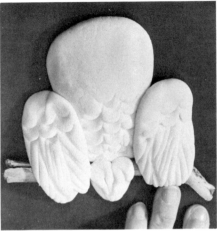

D

E

D. The wings are scalloped at the top with the pill bottle and the bottom feathers cut and lifted with the tip of a paring knife.

E. The wings are placed on the body and over the twig, as shown.

F. Next, the topknot, also scalloped, is placed across the head.

G. The two balls are flattened and scored at the edges for the eye sockets.

H. The pods and pebble are pushed into place. Add a wire loop on the back of the head; bake at 300° about 2 hours, glazing, if desired, to achieve different shades for wings and body. Or paint overall when cool.

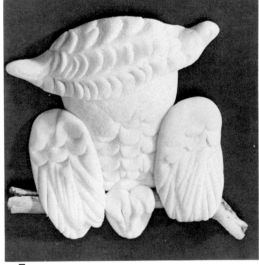

F

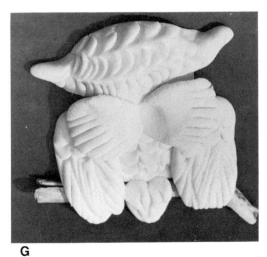

G

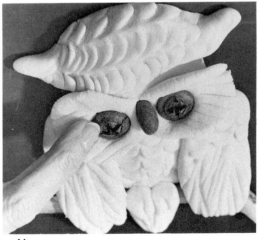

H

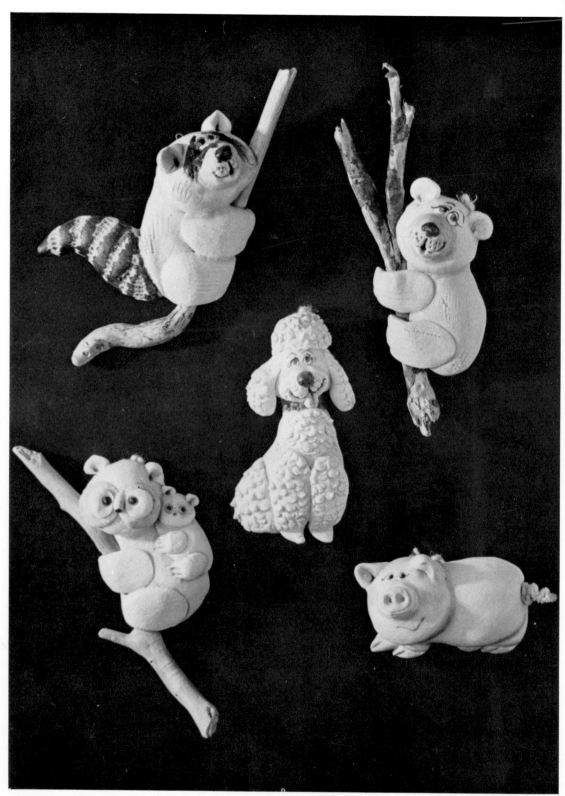

Above: Assorted animals by Virginia Black are created in the same series of steps as shown in the owl. Analyze how the shapes can be broken down into circles and ovals, and then simply assemble the parts and decorate in your own style.

Opposite top: The same principles of design and construction are employed by Kathie Fujisaka to create the running dog. The body and head are shaped and combined; legs, tail, ears, nose, tongue, and other details are each individual pieces of dough added over the original body and head shapes.

Opposite center: Three tiny bears by Laura Zambo are about the height of an adult's thumb and very delicately painted. All are made from simple balls and coils of dough.

Opposite below: By Kathie Fujisaka. The horse and rider are made by assembling geometric shapes.

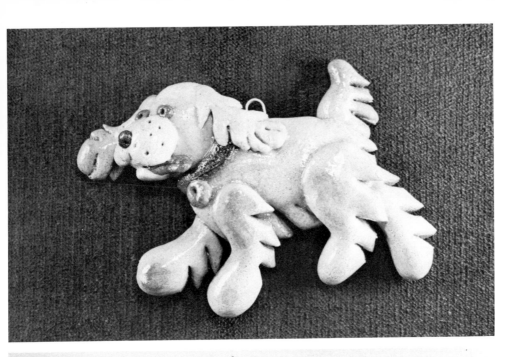

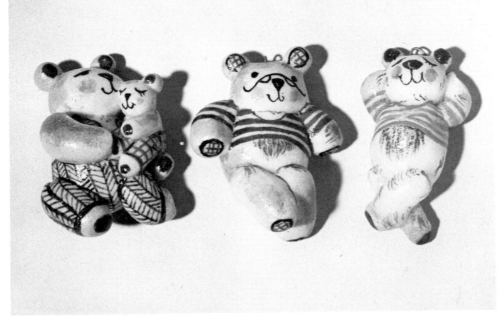

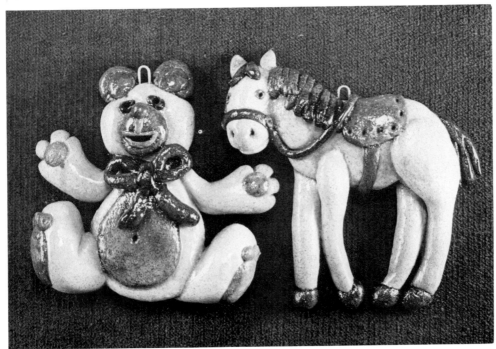

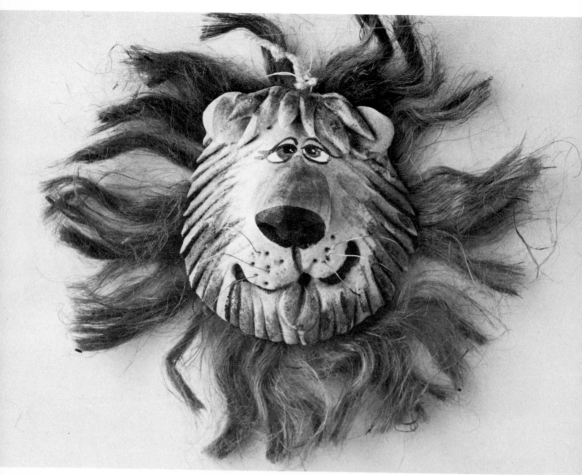

Virginia Black combines a jute fringe and wire whiskers to make a lion head that is loaded with personality.

Materials include the ball of dough, brass wire and wire cutter, wire for hangers and assorted seedpods and shells that she might use for eyes instead of painting them. The shells and pods also are used in other figures shown. The fringe is made from a length of jute shredded and stitched on the sewing machine. It is glued to a cardboard circle and then glued onto the back of the lion. Jute and cardboard are added *after* the piece has been baked, colored, and sealed.

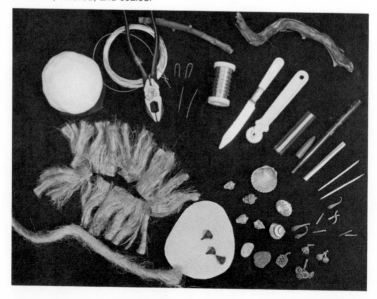

HOW TO CREATE THE LION HEAD

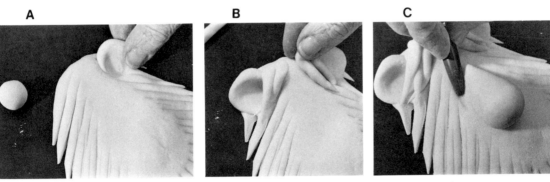

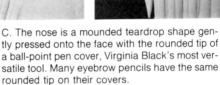

A. A large ball of dough is shaped for the head. Edges are slashed into with a knife for the mane. A small ball is flattened and indented with the thumb for each ear.

B. Additional "mane" is placed between the ears. It is made of thin coils rolled with pointed tips and folded in half.

C. The nose is a mounded teardrop shape gently pressed onto the face with the rounded tip of a ball-point pen cover, Virginia Black's most versatile tool. Many eyebrow pencils have the same rounded tip on their covers.

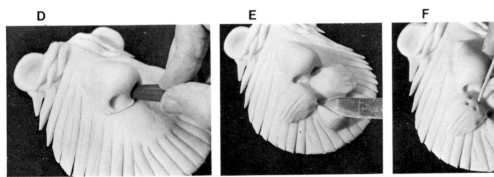

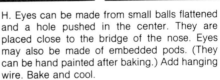

D. Nostrils are pushed in with the same tool.

E. The lips are made from two more dough balls shaped and the edges cut. A tongue is a grooved ball of dough placed between the lips.

F. Whisker indentations can be made with a thin, round stick or a toothpick.

G. Two-inch lengths of brass wire are cut and pushed into the whisker holes.

H. Eyes can be made from small balls flattened and a hole pushed in the center. They are placed close to the bridge of the nose. Eyes may also be made of embedded pods. (They can be hand painted after baking.) Add hanging wire. Bake and cool.

I. The fringe is created by gluing the stitched jute around the cardboard cut to the same shape as the lion's head. The cardboard and mane are glued onto the back.

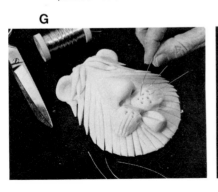

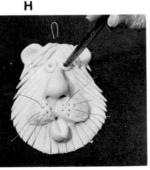

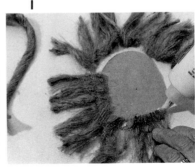

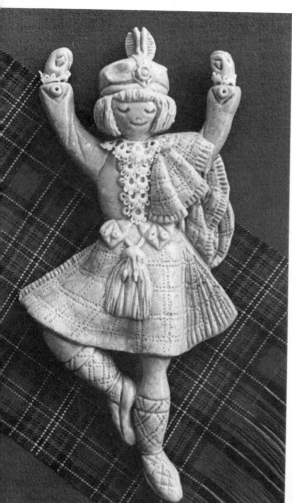

CREATING DANCING FIGURES

The figures and demonstration on these pages are by Marian Gault, who creates authentic costumes for dancers from various countries. Each is built up with shapes of dough in essentially the same manner one would create a doll from stuffed materials. She often sketches the doll first. *(All photos by Ned Gault)*

Left: A Scottish dancer with real lace added around neck and sleeves.

Below left: A Tyrolean figure approximately 4″ high.

Below: A Macedonian dancer, about 8″ high, shown after baking. The painted and varnished figure can be seen in the color section.

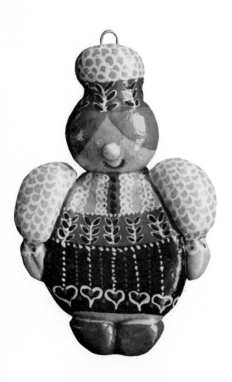

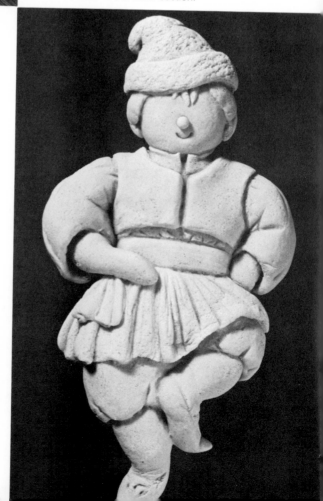

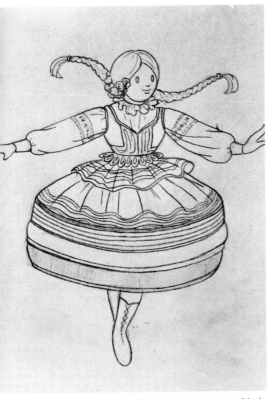

Pencil sketch of a dancer in a costume of Lublin, Poland.

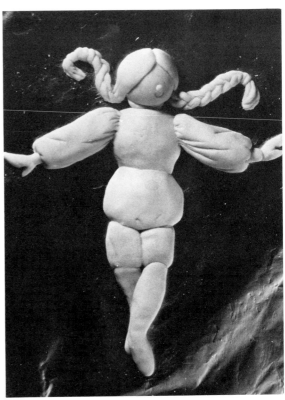

Begin with a ball of dough for the head; add shapes for the neck, torso, arms, hands, and hair.

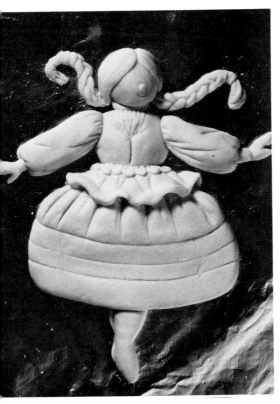

Skirt and peplum shapes are flattened, then placed over the body. The bodice is designed by impressing. Flattened, indented balls are arranged for the belt.

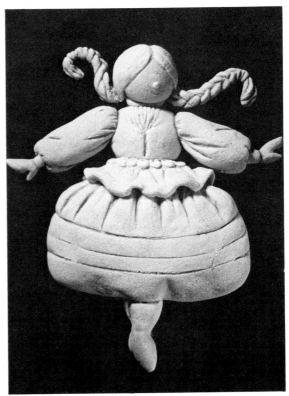

After baking, the dough tends to expand, or puff up slightly. This can often enhance the shape and make it look rounder. Any imperfections can be camouflaged with painting (see finished figure in color section).

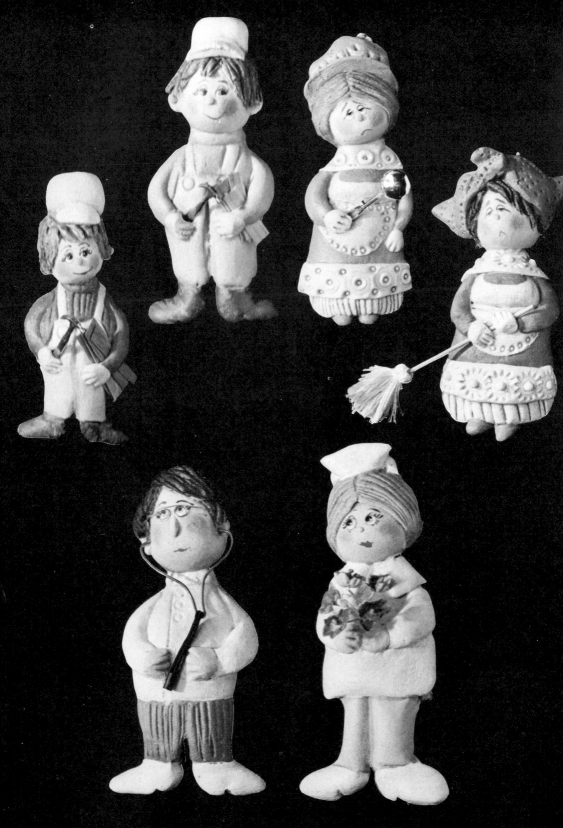

Assorted figures by Virginia Black. Each is about 6″ high. Two handymen, two tired housewives, a physician and a nurse who hold actual objects. The broom handle is made from a lollipop stick with yarn bristles added after baking. Miniature objects such as the potato scoop, stethoscope, and flowers are sold in craft shops. The doctor's glasses are formed with looped brass wire. Metal, wood, and some plastic objects can be baked in low oven temperatures (under 300°).

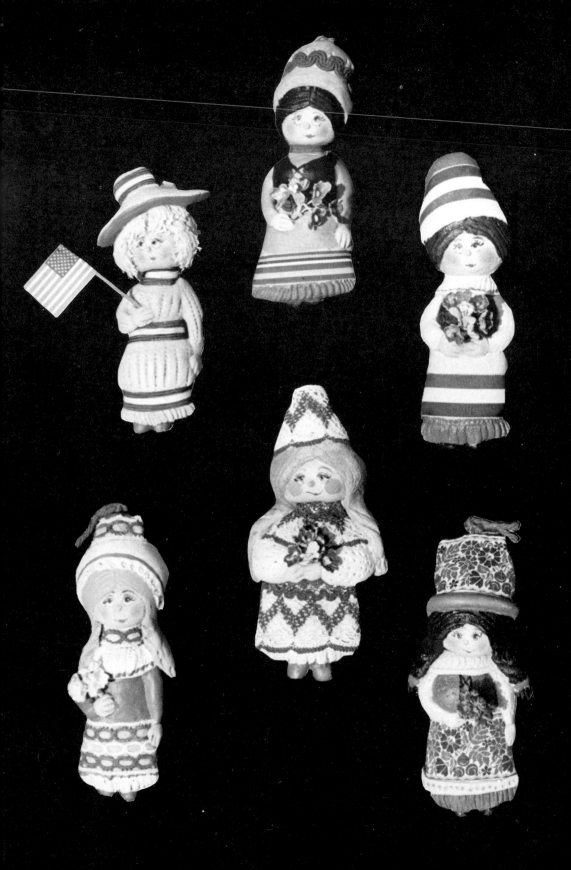

Patriotic ladies by Virginia Black carry flowers and flags. Their skirts and hats are decorated with real pieces of ribbon and laces glued over the baked, painted, and matte-varnished dough figures. Observe and practice the few simple paint lines used to create the eyes and mouths with a fine paintbrush and acrylic colors. Cream cosmetic rouge is dabbed on the cheeks.

MAKING A MERMAID

Virginia Black shares her method of creating a
mermaid that can only be termed darling and
adorable, a delight to hang as a decoration any-
where.

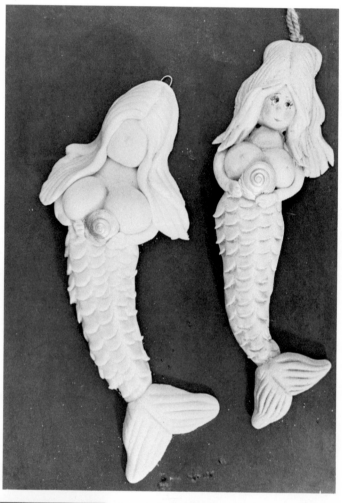

An unbaked mermaid *(left)*. At right, after baking, finishing and sealing with a matte varnish.
The seashell is real.

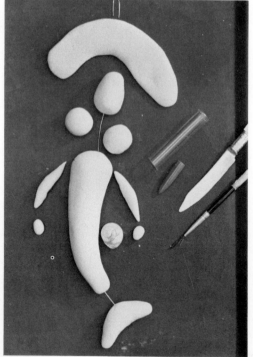

The following shapes are used to make the mermaid. The body and tail are strengthened by
adding a length of wire (or toothpick) between
the parts. Parts used are *(from top to bottom):*
hair, head, bosom, body, arms, hands, shell,
and tails. Virginia's ever-present glass tube,
pen-point tip, paring knife, and water brush are
the only tools she uses. Facial features are added with a fine paintbrush.

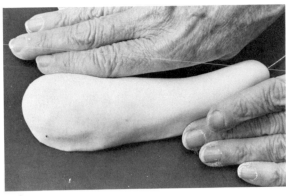

A. The body is shaped.

B. A short piece of any thin wire is pushed into the bottom of the body and the tail. Water must always be brushed onto the touching parts to adhere.

A

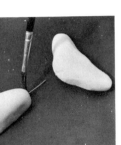

B

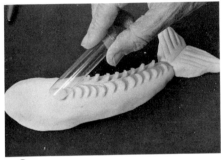

C

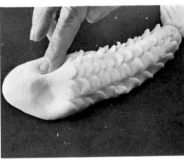

D

C. The tail is scored with the knife and the fins made with the edge of the glass tube partway up the body to the waist.

D. Indentations are made with the finger where the bosom will be set.

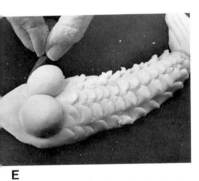

E

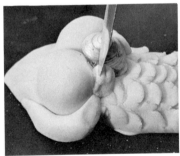

F

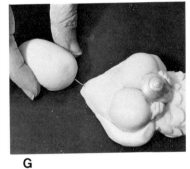

G

E. After moistening the indentations, the bosom is pushed into place and the edges sealed to the body with the penholder tip.

F. The seashell is placed beneath the bosom and the arms and hands added.

G. The head is placed onto the neck with the wire support added between.

H. The hairpiece is scored with a knife.

I. The head is moistened and the hair arranged in place over head and shoulders.

J. After baking rock hard, the features are painted, the hair colored, and lhe body tinted with light blues and greens.

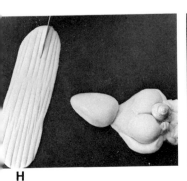

H

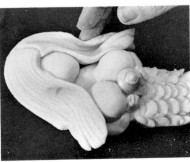

I

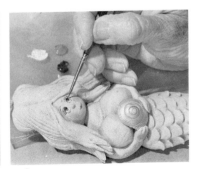

J

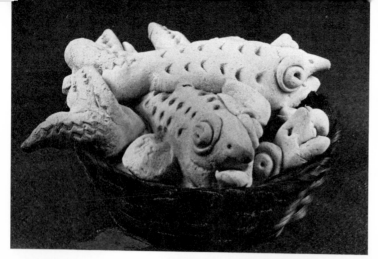

Above: A basket of fish by Barbara Herberholz shows another way to make scales and tails. The fish is shaped from one piece of dough with eyes added. *(Courtesy, artist)*

Right: Neptune riding an ornate water dragon has been created by Wally Remington. The piece is 7″ long. *(Photo, Barbara Herberholz)*

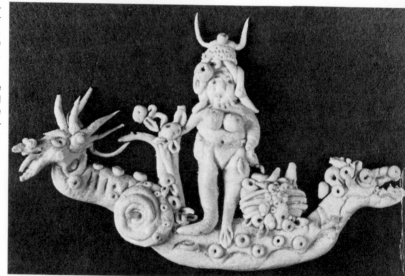

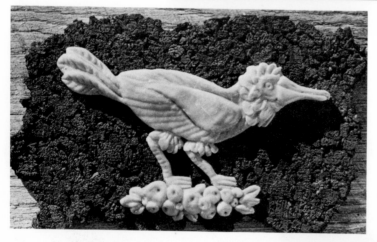

Above: Natural baked color, highly glazed bird by Lois Crachy is mounted on ragged-edge cork within a weathered-wood frame.

Right: Horse, finished as above, by Lois Crachy on a framed cork square.

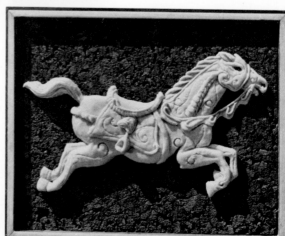

Top: By Gretchen McCarthy. Colored and natural baker's clay ornaments and mirror on a painted pink shaped plywood backing. (*Courtesy, artist*)

Below: By Chantal. Painted baker's clay mounted on a black wood backing. The hat is a lid from a small jar glued onto the dough after baking.

Top: By Linda Fugate. Pink ruffled miniature doll, 2 ½″ high, exquisitely made from the bread and glue recipe.

Below: By Bernice A. Houston. Red, red roses. Bread and glue recipe fashioned over wrapped wire stems.

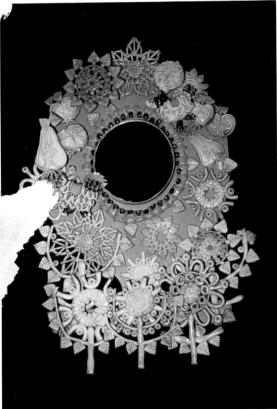

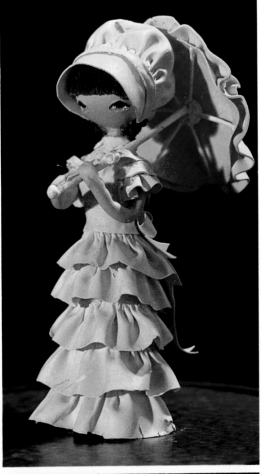

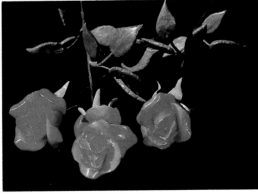

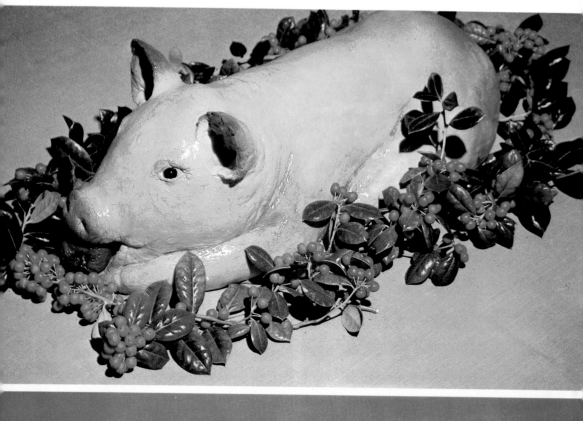
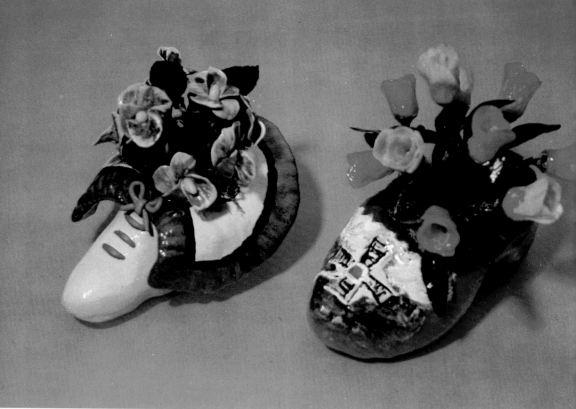

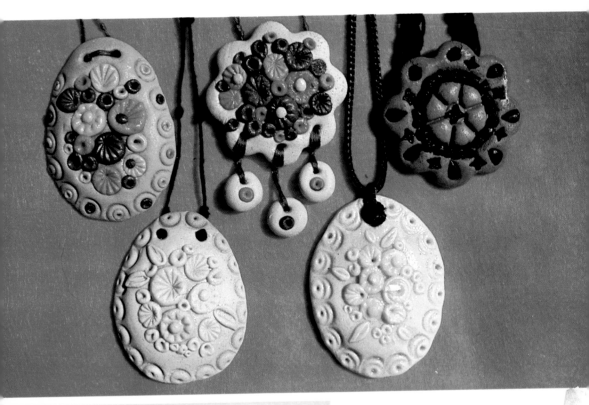

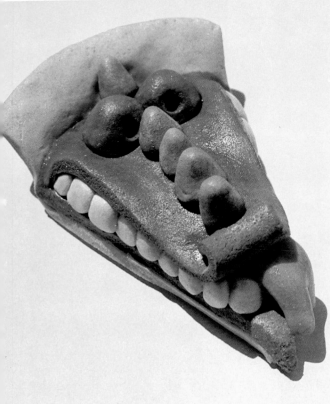

Opposite:

Top: By Melenie Loosli. Suckling-pig center-piece 7″ high, 22″ long, 10″ wide. Made over an armature of coffee and juice cans wired together, then covered with foil. Six basic baker's clay recipes were used. A foil ball was placed between jaws to hold mouth open during baking. Baking time was 10 hours starting at 200° and gradually raising to 350° for browning the egg-white glaze. (*Courtesy, artist*)

Bottom: By Lotte Hunt. Dutch shoes of baker's clay with flowers made from bread and glue dough.

Above: By Maureen Jillie. Baker's clay cut out with cookie cutters, then decorated by adding on circles and other shapes and by imprinting designs. (*Courtesy, Barbara Herberholz*)

Left: By Julia Marshall. "Monster Pie" made from baker's clay, precolored with watercolors. After baking, a polyureathane varnish was brushed on.

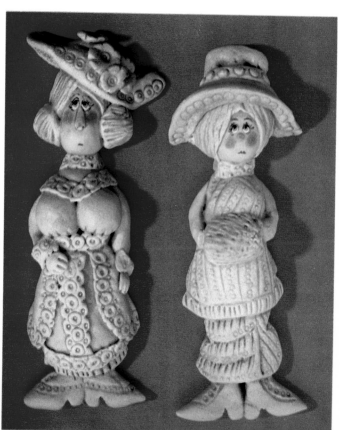

Opposite:

Top left: By Virginia Black. "Lady of the Evening" made of hand-painted baker's clay with silver fabric trim and real feather added.

Top right: By Kay Whitcomb. Leprechaun of hand-painted baker's clay about 10" high with wire reinforcement within.

Bottom: By Marian Gault. Dancers from Lublin and Macedonia in authentically designed, hand-painted costumes. About 6" high. (*Photo, Ned Gault*)

Left: By Virginia Black. Victorian ladies about 9" tall of natural colored baker's clay with hand-painted facial features.

Below: By Chantal. The girl is 11" high and holds an actual jar; the boy is 14" high and holds an aluminum measuring cup.

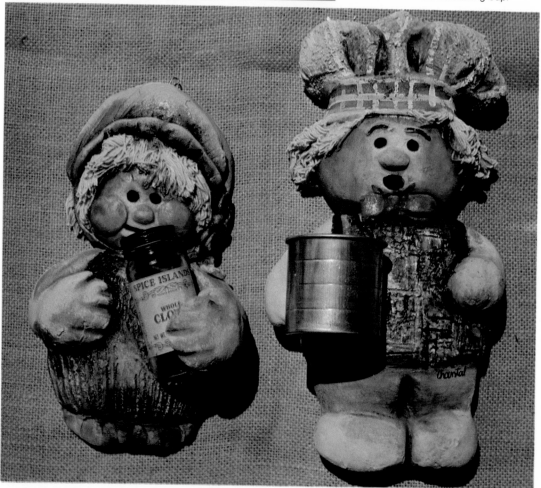

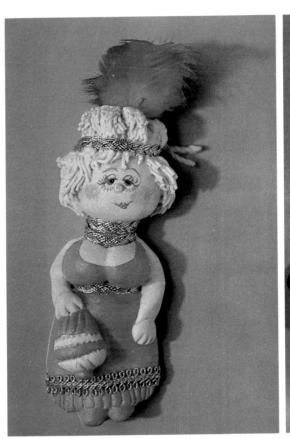

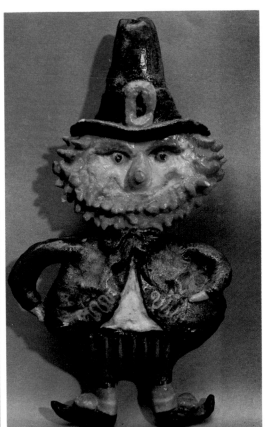

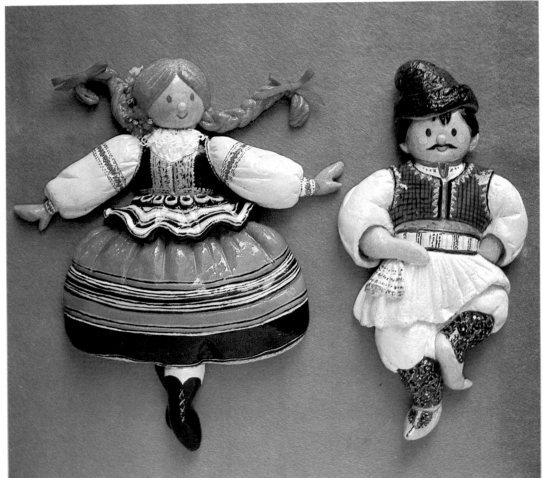

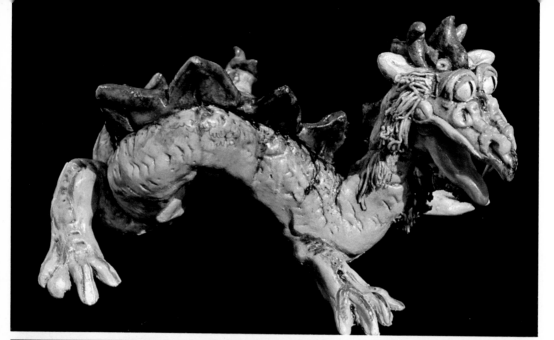

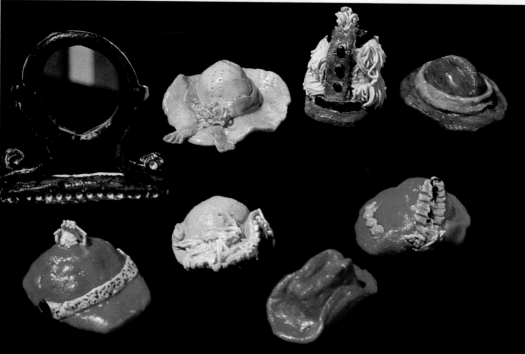

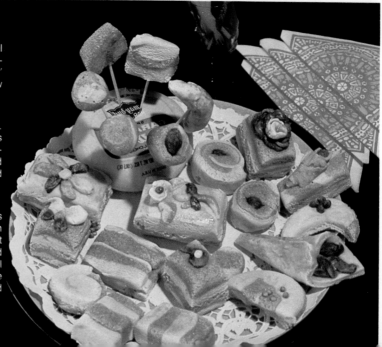

Top: By Pat Smiley. Sculptural dragon is shaped over aluminum foil, 4 1/2″ high, 8 1/2″ wide. The baker's clay is slow baked and hand painted.

Center: By Dona Meilach. "Hat Shoppe." Miniature hats of baker's clay made over aluminum foil with mirror stand made of coiled and rolled shapes.

Right: By Dona Meilach. Hors d'oeuvres. Recipes made with white flour and whole-wheat flour were used and combined in layers to simulate real bread. Decorations were made with paste food coloring added to white dough.

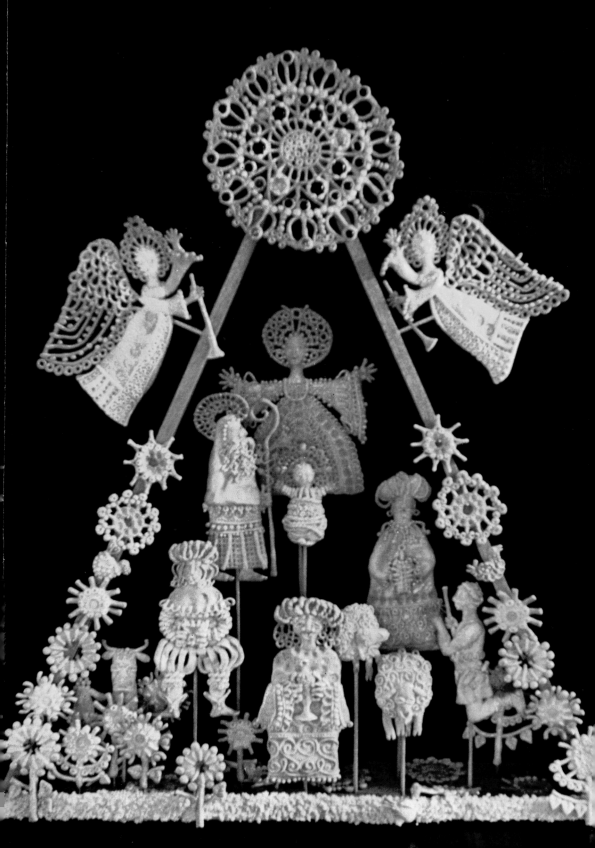

By Gretchen McCarthy. Christmas "tree" made of three slats of wood in a triangle to serve as the base for the ornaments of baker's clay snowflakes, angels, and wise men; some are set on wooden sticks placed in holes in the frame. (*Courtesy, artist*)

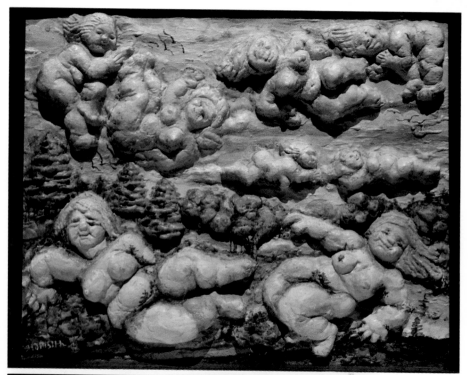

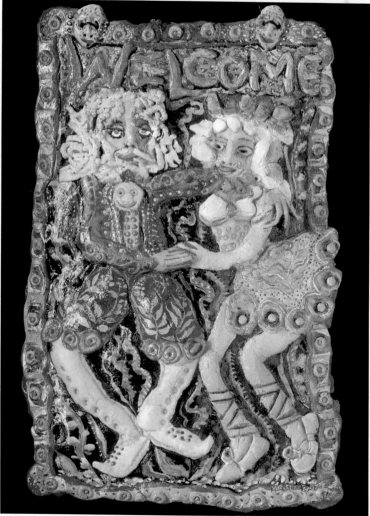

Top: By Arlene Seitzinger. "Woman-scape" 18"
high, 21" wide. Baker's clay ladies, trees, and
clouds were shaped and baked separately, then
assembled on a painted Masonite backing, and
framed.

Below: By Mari Bianca. Richly ornamented
plaque of baker's clay, 10" high, 7 ½" wide,
combines basic circles and coils, imprinted and
hand painted. (*Courtesy, artist*)

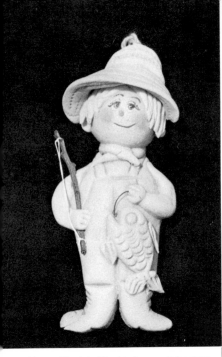

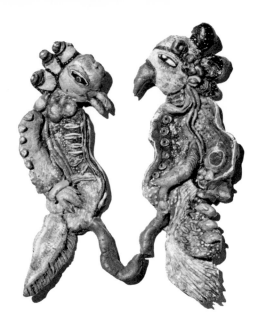

Above: Virginia Black's happy fisherman holds a rod made of a twig and his catch with the wire hook in its mouth.

Above right: Two parrots, brightly colored and varnished. By Mari Bianca.

Right: Kay Whitcomb places mirrors in the tummies of her owls. (See page 51 for use of mirrors.)

Below: A fish mirror. By Kay Whitcomb. The object is decorative and functional.

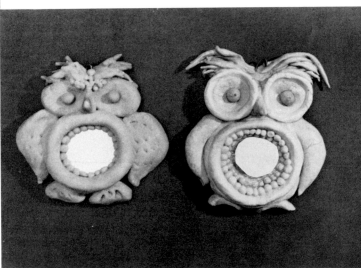

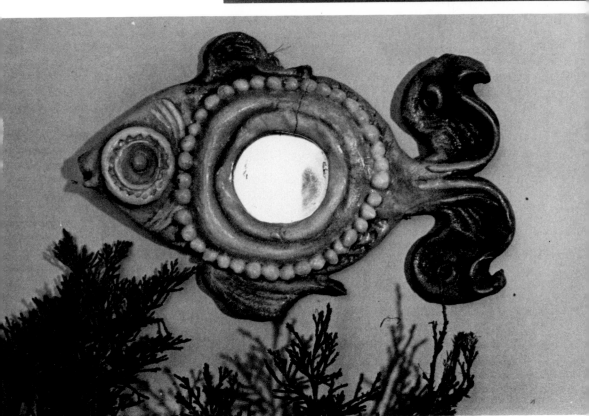

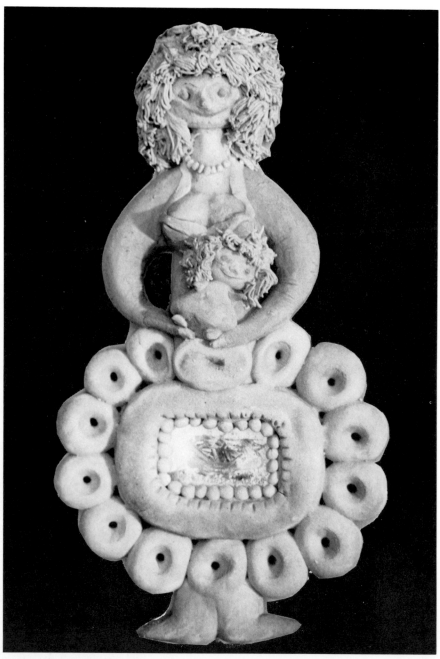

A mother and child, about 11″ high. By Kay Whitcomb.

KAY WHITCOMB CREATES A FIGURE

Kay Whitcomb, a design teacher and internationally known enamelist, combines her talents to show the sculptural and creative potential of bread dough with mirror inlays and wire reinforcements. Mirrors must be backed with aluminum foil and raised off the pan by inlaying them on a coil of dough. If laid flat on the pan, the heat will crack them. Improperly placed mirrors may crack when the dough cools, or the dough may crack. Mirrors can also be glued onto the back of a baked object.

Small mirrors can be purchased in craft and needlework shops and at cosmetic counters. Self-stick mirror squares sold in decorating departments can be cut to shapes with a glass cutter. Objects with mirrors should be baked at temperatures of about 300° or lower. Never glue a fabric backing directly onto the mirror back or the silvering will peel off. Cover back with self-stick paper, and then glue on felt or other fabric.

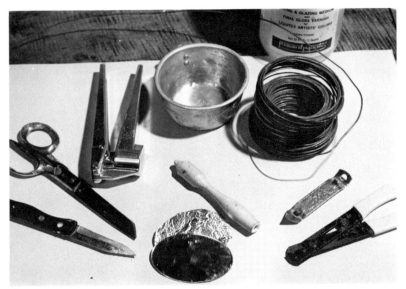

The figure requires one full recipe of dough. Wire (stovepipe or any rust-resistant strong flexible wire about ⅛″ diameter), wire cutters, garlic press, mirror about 4″ wide, piece of aluminum foil cut to size of mirror; the knife, can opener, and wood toy part are used for making designs in the dough.

Laying in the Mirror

A. A coil is rolled and made into an oval. Ends are cut with a knife, then moistened and pushed together.

B. The aluminum foil is placed behind the mirror. . .

C. . . . and laid onto the center of the coil. This holds the mirror up from the metal baking sheet.

D. It is pushed down into the coil. . .

E. . . . and the top of the coil brought around over the mirror edge gently.

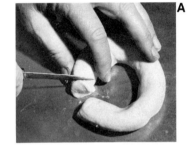

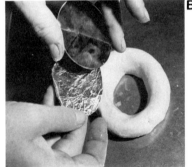

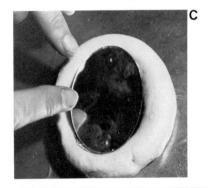

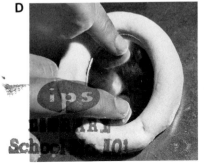

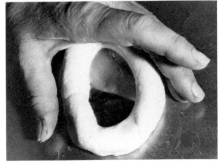

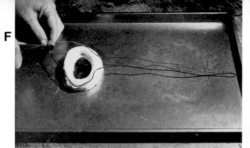

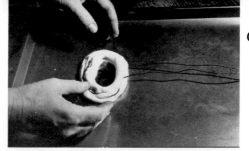

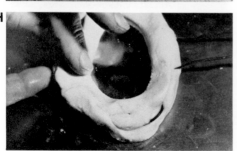

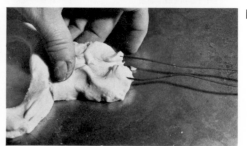

Laying in the Support Wire

F. A length of wire is folded so it serves as a hanger device at the top and as an interior strengthening wire through the torso and bottom of the piece.

G. The bottom of the wire is arranged around the oval with ends extending into the feet.

H. It is thoroughly embedded under the dough around the mirror.

I. Dough pieces, handled as clay, are laid along the wire upward.

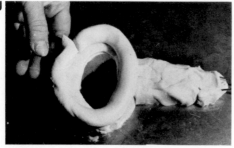

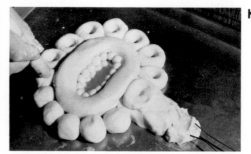

J. Another coil is then rolled and laid on top of the original coil. It is adhered by moistening with water.

K. Small circles are laid around the border of the mirror; large circles around the outer edge are indented with the wooden peg from a child's carom board game.

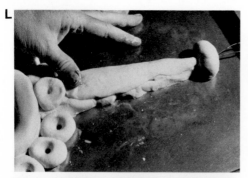

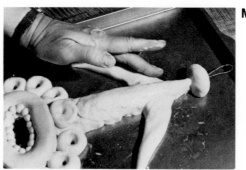

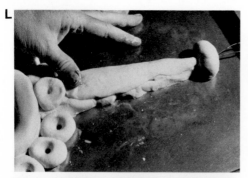

L. A flattened length of dough is placed over the torso wire, and a flattened ball becomes the basis for the head.

M. Arms are added out to the sides.

N. A bosom is placed on the torso in the same line as the arms.

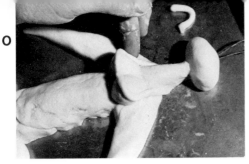

O. A thin coil laid over the bosom becomes a dress neckline.

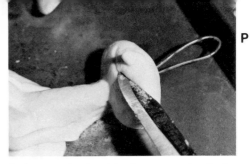

P. A groove is placed for the nose and a short piece of shaped dough added over it. The mouth is shaped with the curved top of the paring-knife blade and mouth corners pushed up with the thumbs to create a smile. Eyes are made with the wood toy tool.

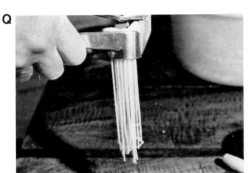

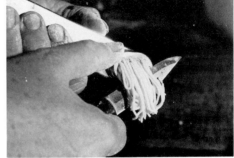

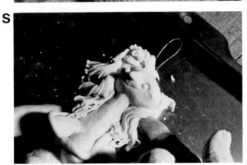

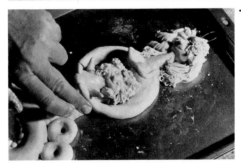

Q. Hair is made by pressing through the garlic press. For longer hair simply add more dough and keep pressing.

R. Cut hair to desired length, moisten head and. . .

S. . . . design a pleasing coiffure.

T. The child is created on the mother's body and the mother's arms are bent to hold the baby.

U. The finished figure is ready to be baked for about 3 to 4 hours.

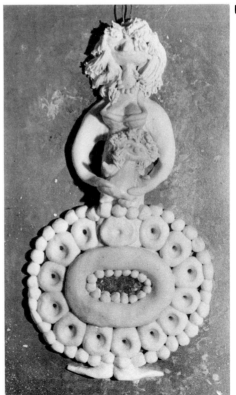

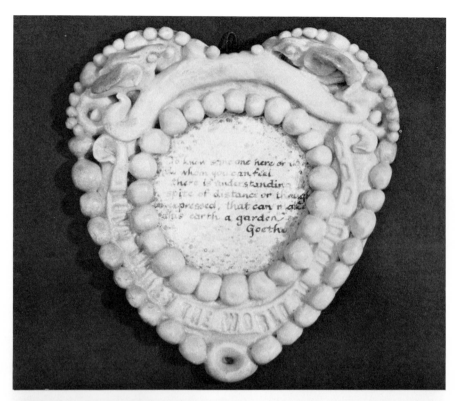

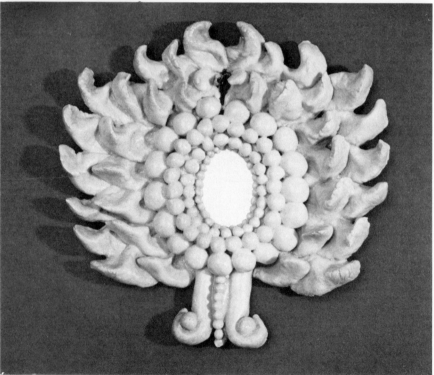

A bread-dough valentine *(above)* and the mirror tree *(below)* by Kay Whitcomb are constructed by the same method as shown in the preceding demonstration. The inlaid pieces are placed on coils, and wire supports are wrapped within.

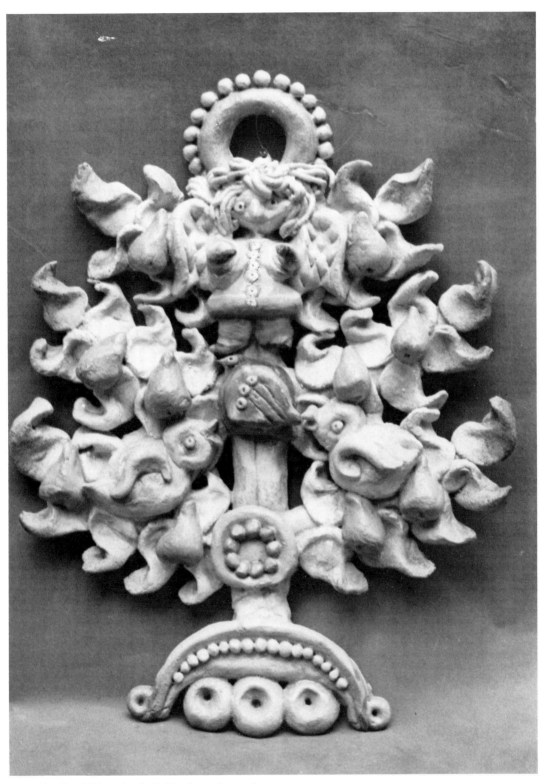

By Kay Whitcomb. A highly decorative wall-
hanging piece, brilliantly colored and inspired
by Mexican candleholders.

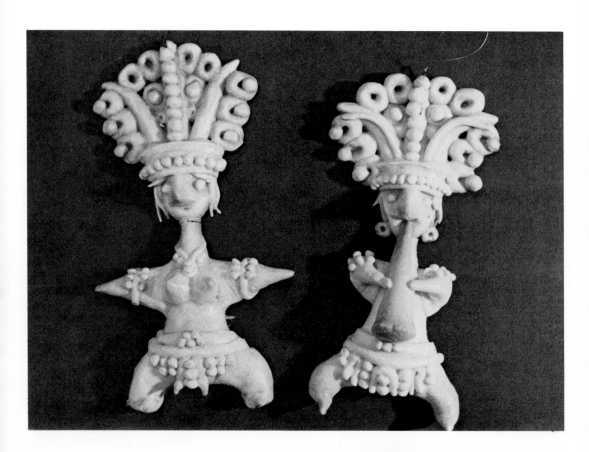

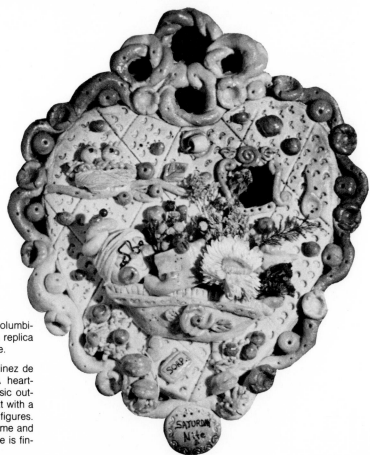

Above: By Kay Whitcomb. Two pre-Columbian figures inspired this bread-dough replica used for a wedding table centerpiece.

Right: Saturday Night. By Rita Martinez de Blake (Mama's Cookie Factory). A heart-shaped cake pan is used for the basic outline. The heart shape is rolled out flat with a rolling pin, then embellished with figures. Coils and circles are used for the frame and dried flowers glued on after the piece is finished.

56

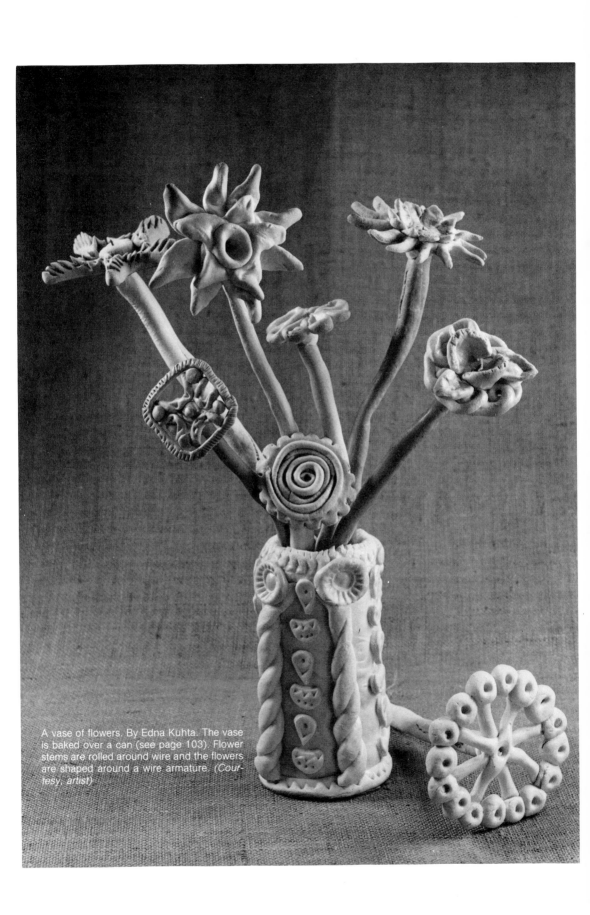

A vase of flowers. By Edna Kuhta. The vase is baked over a can (see page 103). Flower stems are rolled around wire and the flowers are shaped around a wire armature. (Courtesy, artist)

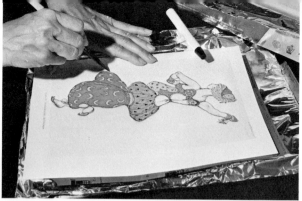

A

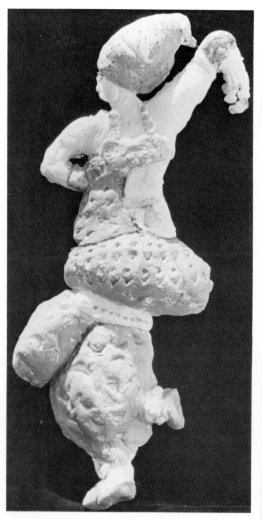

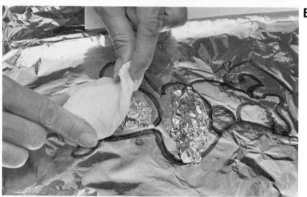

B

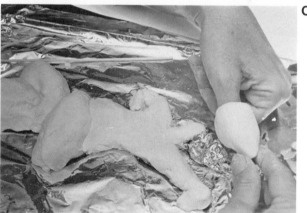

C

SHAPING OVER FOIL

Many forms can be shaped over aluminum foil crushed into shapes. The result is a lightweight delicate-looking figure with a thin shell that bakes quickly. The following series shows the use of foil and a method for designing a figure over a drawing.

A. A design can be original or one that is traced onto a sheet of foil laid on a baking sheet.

B. Balls of foil of different sizes and heights are shaped onto portions of the drawing needed for the thickest parts of the figure.

C. Shaped pieces of dough are laid over the balls and worked within the traced outline. The hat is shaped over the thumb and laid onto the mounded piece of foil.

D. The figure is embellished with the costume design.

E. After baking, the foil is removed from the back; the figure can be baked a little longer after the foil is out to be sure it is thoroughly dry.

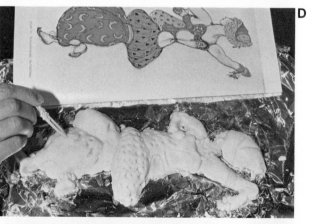

D

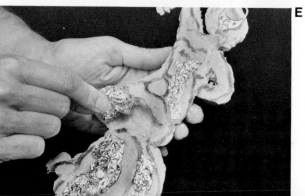

E

Right: Head by Pat Smiley is formed around a ball of foil. Long kneading of the dough in small pieces results in the ceramic-like texture that is achieved. The piece was placed on a wood skewer stuck into a bowl of sand so it would have no flat sides to it and baked very slowly.

Below: Eggs by Rita Martinez de Blake are shaped around foil. If foil was not used, the eggs would be too solid to bake through; they might puff up and bubble.

Bottom: Hats by Dona Meilach. Each hat was formed over a foil core (see color section).

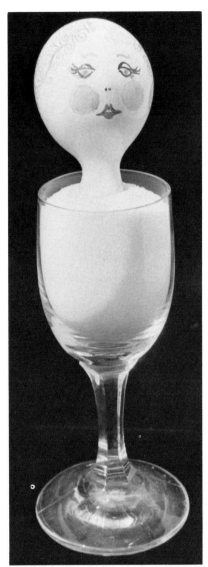

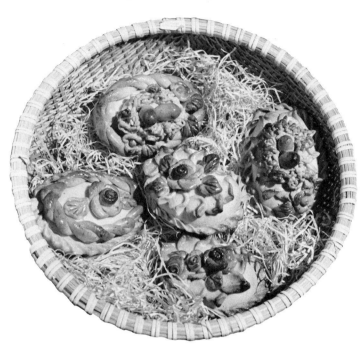

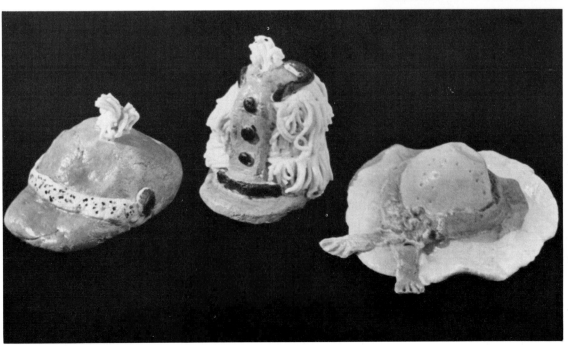

59

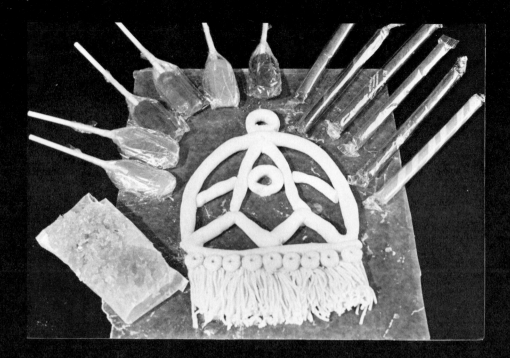

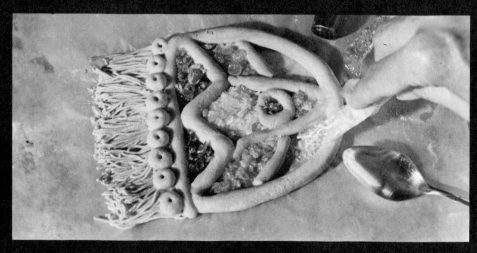

CREATING STAINED GLASS EFFECTS

A Tiffany lamp utilizing the effect of stained glass can be achieved with bread dough. The "leading" or outline must be made first and kept as flat as possible during baking. When it is thoroughly baked, place the piece on a sheet of waxed paper and add crushed colored candies into the empty spaces. Bake about 10 minutes, or until the candy melts. Cool thoroughly. Leave the waxed paper behind the entire object as the candy remains sticky and the waxed paper serves as a backing. The piece can be hung as an ornament or where light can be seen through it in front of a window. Its permanence is questionable because the candy cannot be thoroughly sealed with varnish. Colored candies can also be melted within indentations of a piece for another effect.

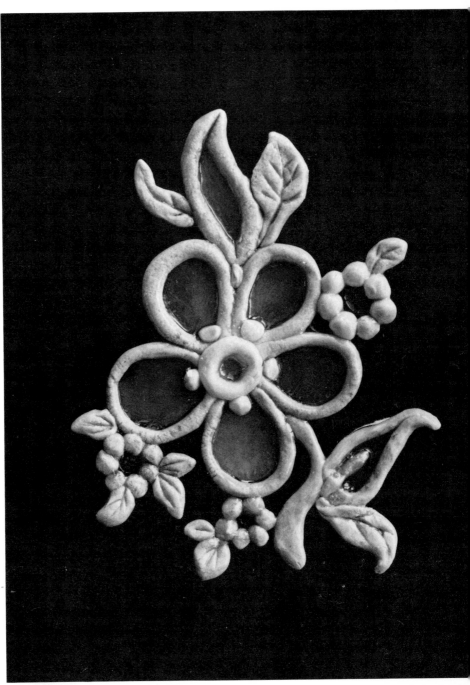

Flower by Marian Gault in natural colors
with clear candy in petals and leaves.
(Photo, Ned Gault)

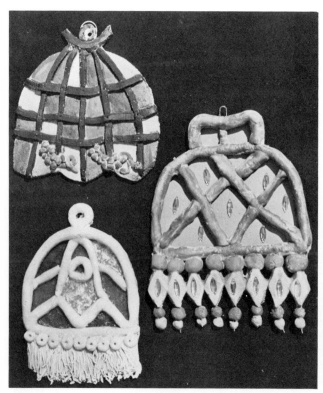

The finished candy-filled Tiffany lamp (*bottom, left*) and two similar lamp decorations are shown here. By Dona Meilach. The same principles apply to butterflies, flowers, windows in buildings, baskets, and for jewelry.

A. The backing for the lamp (top left) is rolled out with a rolling pin (see page 66) and cut to shape. Another rolled-out portion is cut into narrow strips.

B. Vertical strips are placed on the lamp backing and cut.

C. Horizontal strips are laid across and woven into the verticals. Dough should be quite stiff so strips do not stretch and tear.

D. A grape cluster is added at each scallop point and a circle at the top. The circle is held to the lamp with a toothpick inserted as shown at right. A soft-drink can tab is placed behind the circle so that all the hanging weight will not be on the bread-dough circle.

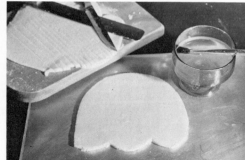

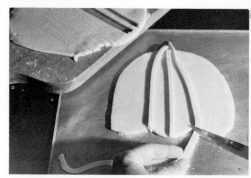

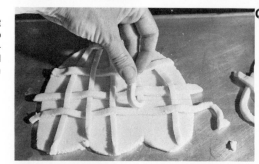

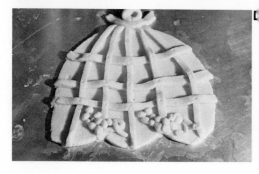

Lamp on opposite page, right, is made from coils and blue glass beads combined with precolored green balls. After baking, a piece of green paper was cut to the shape of the lamp and glued to the back; glass beads were glued onto the paper within each diamond space.

A. The diamond-shape beads are laid onto a piece of dough, flattened to about 3/8" and the dough is cut into diamond shapes that are larger than the bead.

B. Diamonds and beads are strung onto a length of wire and inserted into the bottom of the lamp.

C. Toothpicks are inserted into the coils at all connecting points to prevent the dough from shrinking and pulling apart after cooling.

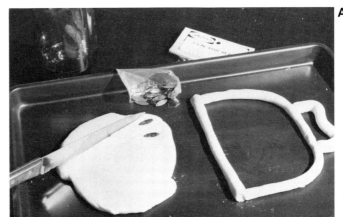

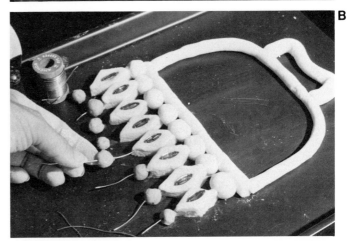

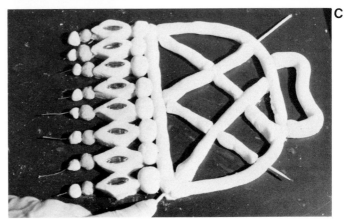

Art Deco fashions and the elongated look of the 1930s inspired this sinuous flowing figure made from flat dough with only slight raised areas. By Allen Meilach.

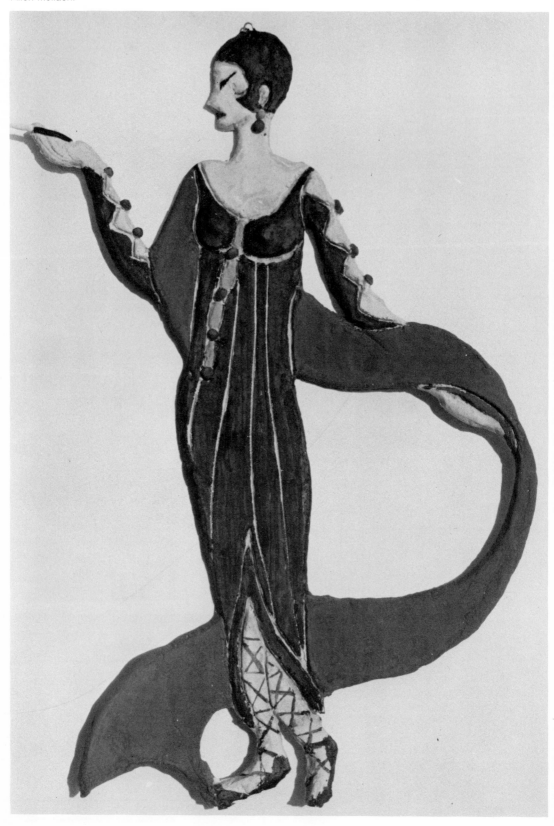

5
THE FLAT DESIGN

A flat sheet of dough, rolled out with a rolling pin or a glass jar, offers another challenging approach to bread-dough design. With a sheet of dough as a backing surface, you can build up layers and layers of pattern in almost the same way you would think of adding layers of fabric in appliqué. The finished object can be in low or high relief and take advantage of shadows falling within the parts for some of its appeal. You could readily emulate something as complex as the ancient, deeply cut stone frieze on the Parthenon or the tiny carved ivories made by the early Romans.

Sheets of dough should be used about ¼" to ½" thick; thin sheets tend to warp in baking. Thinner pieces can be used (see the wreaths, page 116) if the dough is well kneaded, and other shapes are built up and attached by poking an instrument through the layers as well as by moistening.

Air bubbles trapped in rolled dough that appear during baking occur when dough has been improperly or insufficiently kneaded. Sometimes when you make an object, change your mind, then refold and reroll the dough without kneading it again, air bubbles will be present and emerge when the dough is baked.

Watch the baked object carefully; and if air bubbles arise, poke them with a pin or toothpick and place a heavy object over them to weight and flatten. Sometimes the elusive bubbles recur during the cooling and drying process. This may happen if the piece has not been sufficiently baked. There are possible remedies: (1) Place the piece in a damp spot such as the bathroom until the bubble is moist enough to poke with a pin without cracking the dough, then rebake with a weight on it. (2) Sometimes just reheating it will soften it sufficiently to poke it and weight down. (3) Leave the bubble in the piece and use it inventively to enhance the design where possible. (4) Use an automatic sander to smooth out the bump . . . very carefully if possible. (5) If a dent is left, try patching by adding a piece of dough and rebaking, then sanding in any edges, or excise the dough and bake in a patch of new dough. (6) When all else fails, scrap the piece and use it for testing colors and finishes.

Rolled-out dough can be combined with forms made with coils and circles, and shapes can be made with cookie cutters (see page 89). Large plaques can be backed with screen wire, pegboard, or Masonite (as in chapter 8).

The flat pattern is adaptable to the double-bake process (see pages 70, 71, and 72). This enables you to have pockets and other pieces that stand away from the background or to build up layers that would otherwise be too heavy for the moist dough to support. One could simulate a tiered wedding cake or an entire architectural structure. Connecting rods such as toothpicks or wires should be baked in for supporting additional sections of dough. Without them, the pieces can contract and separate as they cool.

Double baking involves designing and baking one layer until it has a crust, or even completely baking it and then adding layers. Subsequent layers do not have to be added immediately. You can add on pieces days, weeks, or months after a first piece is built provided it has not been sealed with varnishes.

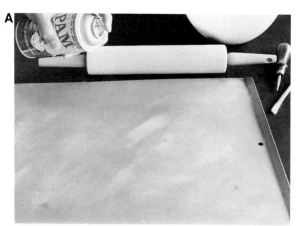

THE ART DECO GIRL

The following demonstration by Allen Meilach shows the development of the Art Deco girl on the preceding page and can be adapted to many kinds of flat design.

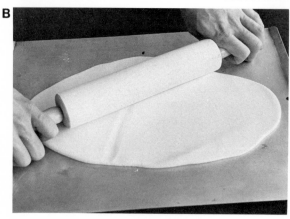

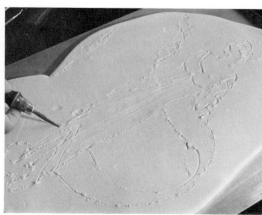

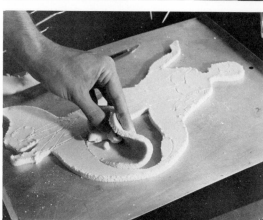

A. Grease, flour, or spray the cookie sheet with a nonstick vegetable oil so pressure of rolling the dough does not cause it to adhere to pan.

B. Knead dough thoroughly to remove air bubbles and roll out with a rolling pin about the size of the cookie sheet and about 3⁄8″ to 1⁄2″ thick.

C. Outline the design on the smoothly rolled dough.

D. Cut away and remove the negative areas.

E. Shape the raised portions and adhere with water.

F. The hair is flat pattern laid on as an appliqué.

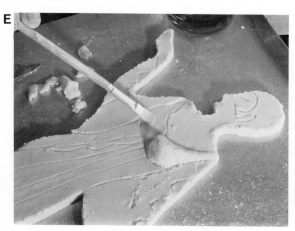

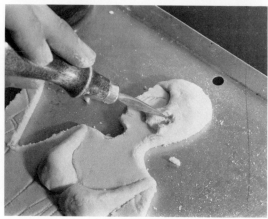

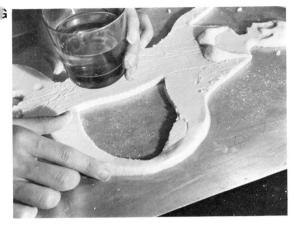

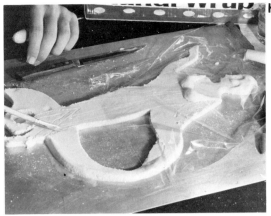

G. Edges are smoothed with a dampened finger.

H. If a portion begins to dry too quickly, cover with plastic wrap.

I. Smooth out design lines with a tool.

J. The delicate protruding cigarette is held solid by wrapping the dough around a piece of toothpick.

K. Buttons and final details are added. If the dough is too moist in some areas or you want to predry it before baking, you can use a hair blower. During baking, the figure developed a bubble that was pricked with a pin, then a metal knife handle was placed over the area to flatten it during additional baking. The piece was baked about 3 hours at 275°.

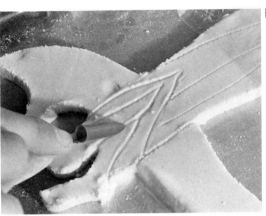

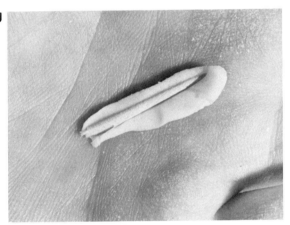

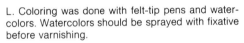

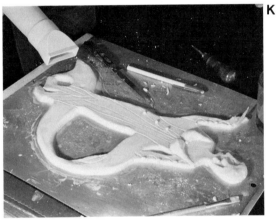

L. Coloring was done with felt-tip pens and water-colors. Watercolors should be sprayed with fixative before varnishing.

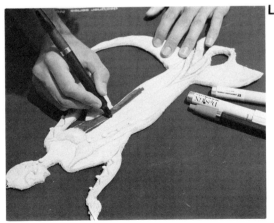

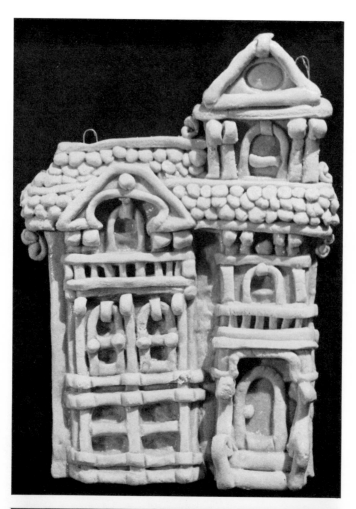

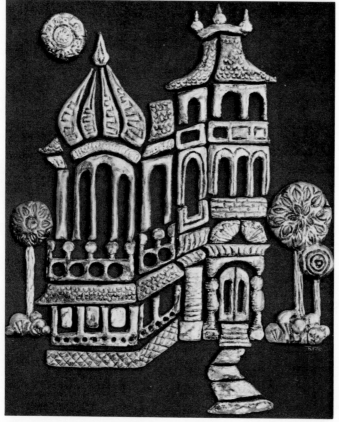

Opposite top: House by Barbara J. Sweetser combines a flat back and cut strips with coils and circles.

Opposite bottom: House by Rosemary Fee. Parts are cut from a flat rolled-out sheet of dough, designed and placed with spacing between them to give a mosaic effect. The parts are glued to a wood panel.

Below: Rosemary Fee. An abstract mosaic made from flat shapes glued to a backing. Rosemary uses three coats of polyurethane varnish, then paints her pieces and antiques them, finishing with three coats of a resin spray.

Right: Edna Kuhta. Hanging decoration combines a flat backing with assembled shaped pieces. *(Courtesy, artist)*

Below right: Landscape with graveyard. By Paul and Sue Krosnick. Approximately 8½″ diameter. Piece is painted with waterproof casein color and dipped in acrylic resin, which produces a high gloss and vivid depth look to the surface.

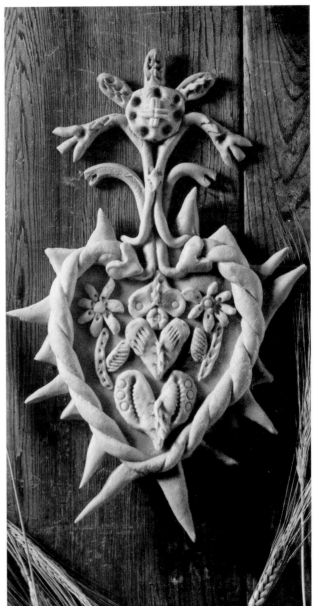

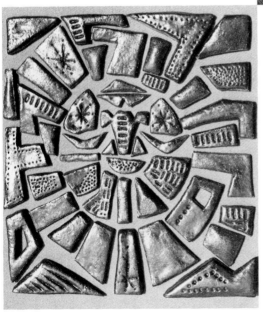

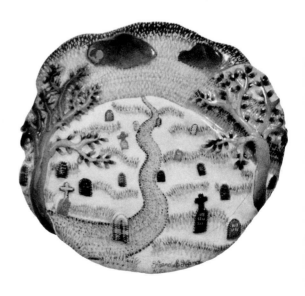

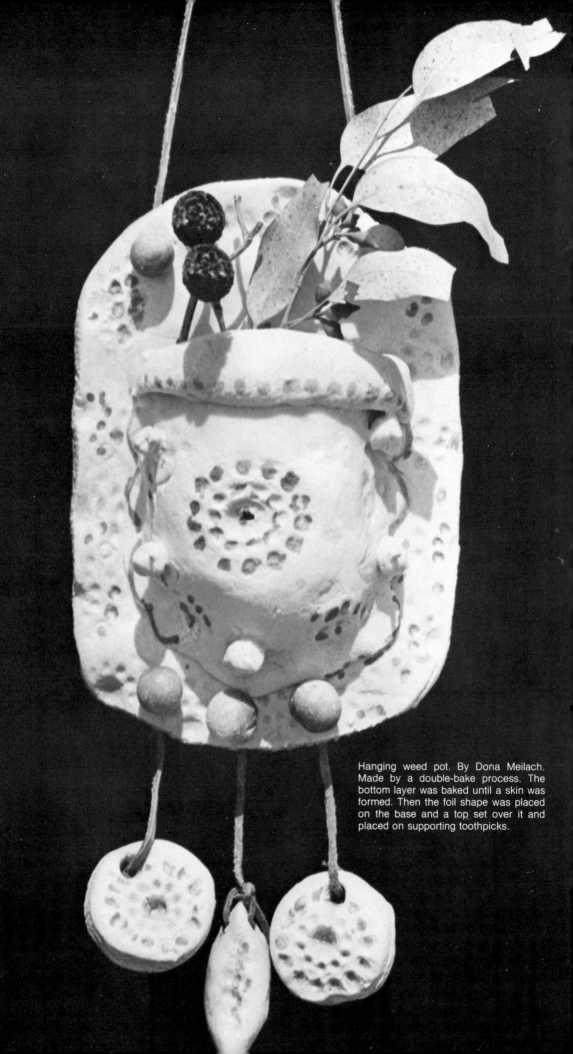

Hanging weed pot. By Dona Meilach. Made by a double-bake process. The bottom layer was baked until a skin was formed. Then the foil shape was placed on the base and a top set over it and placed on supporting toothpicks.

DOUBLE BAKING

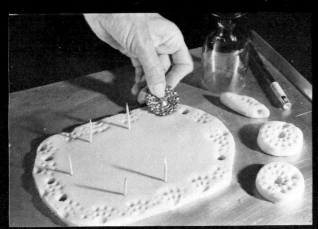

A. Roll the dough to about ½'' thickness. Decide where you want the pouch to go, and stick wooden toothpicks around the pouch area. Make holes for hanging with leather-thonged beads and impress a design around the edge with a decorative button or other instrument. Cut circles and ovals with the rim of a glass to make beads for hanging at bottom of pot. Place in 275° oven and bake about 1½ hours until dough feels hard on top.

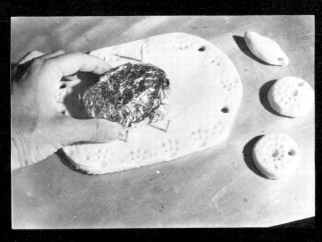

B. Remove from oven and form a foil ball within the toothpick area.

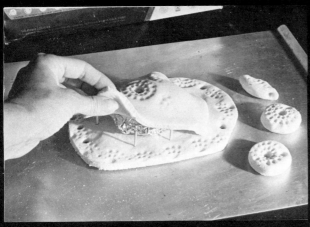

C. Cut another layer of dough the size of the pouch, allowing for shaping. It should be impressed with the design before assembling. Place this layer over the foil and onto the toothpicks, moistening the edge of the dough so it will adhere to the baked layer.

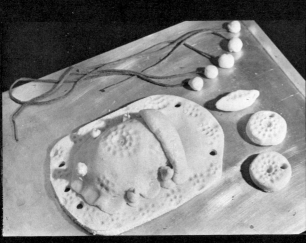

D. Ready for final baking. Place round balls over the tops of the toothpicks for camouflage and design. Wrap ends of leather laces into five additional balls to use as the hanging thongs and provide additional detailing. Leather can easily bake without burning at 275°. Bake 2 to 3 hours more; remove foil and bake at least another hour until entire pot is rock hard. Seal the back with varnish immediately as different drying times of the layers can produce cracking. Color with a brown felt-tip marker. Finish with eight coats of satin varnish and assemble all parts as shown.

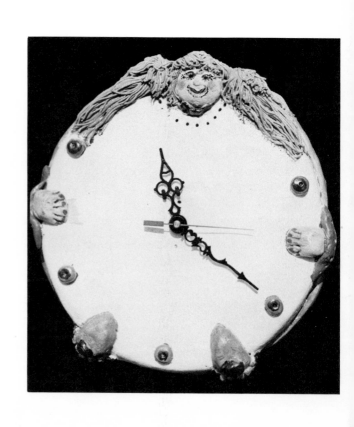

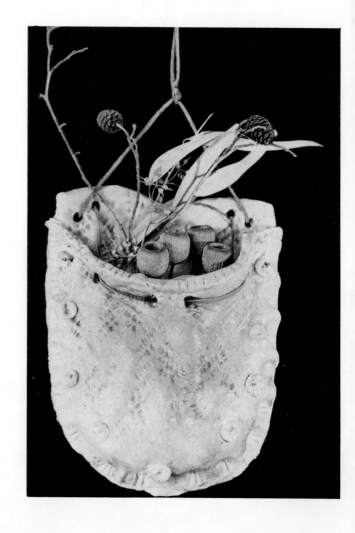

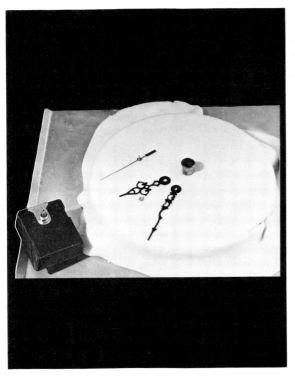

Clock. By Dona Meilach. Place a ⅜″ thick layer of dough over a well-greased upside down 9″ round cake pan. Make a hole the size of the clock's central spindle, and hold open with a thimble or bolt during baking. A battery-operated clock mechanism can be purchased separately. (See Supply Sources.) Decorate the clock's face as shown, or develop your own design. Place a coil around the rim. Bake 4 hours at 275° and watch very carefully. If air bubbles occur, prick with a pin and weight down immediately. A bumpy face can prevent the clock hands from turning properly. Remove from form pan immediately. If inside is not hard when touched with a fingernail, return to oven and bake upside down.

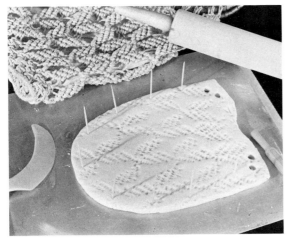

Leather-look weed pot by Dona Meilach. Glazing with egg white the last hour of baking produces a smooth, rich leather appearance.

Roll out the base and create a texture. This one was produced by laying a macramé purse on the dough and pressing it down with the rolling pin. Any highly textured woven fabric pushed against the dough can be used to produce overall textures. Place toothpicks in the first layer to accept pouch. Bake approximately 1½ hours.

For deep, large pouches, use two sections of foil—one balled up for shape, the second laid over the first and used to support the edges. This also makes it easier to remove the foil after the pot is baked. The macramé-purse pattern was rolled onto the top layer and the lip of the pouch shaped. Holes are made to lace the leather hanging thongs through.

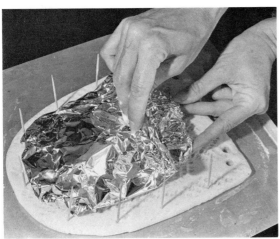

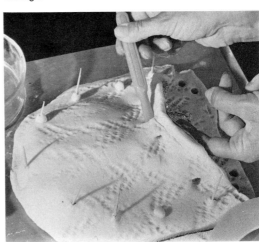

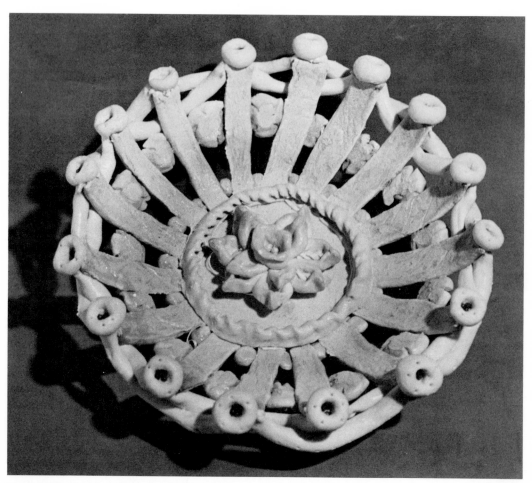

Flower basket by Rita Martinez de Blake is made over a bowl used for a form. After partially baking and removing the form, more decorations are added and the basket rebaked. *(Photographed at the Marco Polo Shop, Santa Fe, New Mexico)*

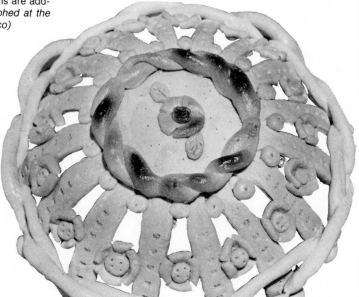

6
BREAD BASKETS

The woven basket, made of bread and used to serve in, has a delightful double meaning. It is probably the object that most people associate with bread-dough art, for craftsmen have been displaying it in quality shops for the past few years.

Bread baskets are made from flat rolled dough, cut into strips for weaving, then shaped either over or within a form (see page 76 for both methods). Forms must be ovenproof bowls or baking pans thoroughly greased with vegetable oil so the dough can be easily removed; they should not have undercuts or rims that will bake within the dough and prevent separating. It is impractical to line a form with aluminum foil to facilitate separating as the foil wrinkles and leaves the wrinkly impressions in the strips.

An average-size basket made over an 8-inch diameter bowl requires about two-thirds of a recipe. Dough should be stiff so the strips do not stretch and tear as they are woven.

When a basket is made over the bottom of an inverted bowl placed on a cookie sheet, the rim is made first and the strips attached to it. The rim that lays flat on the pan is always flat. After baking, it can be decorated by gluing on seeds or objects. It can also be embellished by baking on additional shapes by the double-bake process described in chapter 5. After the basket is hard, remove the form, turn right side up and add balls, cut or molded shapes, or another rim on top of the original, and continue to bake. With practice you can bake the woven strips first, remove the form, turn the hardened strips up, and add the rim, then continue baking.

A basket made by method 2, within the form, is first woven, then the rim added, and decoration applied before baking.

In both methods the strips that lay against the form are plain; to make them interesting, impress designs in the dough before placing them against the form; then design the outer side of the strip before baking. Always add water and impress a tool where the strips meet and overlap. Indentations made by pencil erasers, tools, toothpicks, and so on can be covered with balls, flowers, petals, rosettes, and so forth.

Baskets should be baked at about 275°–300° until hard, then removed from the form, and baking finished right side up. Glaze with any of the methods in chapter 2. Always remove from form to cool.

After you make one or two woven baskets, you will think of many interesting variations. Several ideas are shown using cookie cutters, circles and ovals made with the rims of a small glass, some made solid with painted details added. Add balls and rims for feet and bases. Let your imagination run wild and use the tools you have to suggest other designs.

Always coat baskets with several layers of polyurethane and resin sprays. They should be cleaned with a damp cloth, never immersed in water. If they become soft, they can be rebaked and revarnished.

HOW TO MAKE A WOVEN BASKET

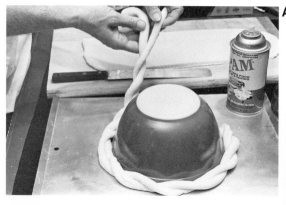

A

Method 1—Over a Form

A. Grease the outside of an ovenproof bowl very well with cooking oil. Place upside down on baking sheet. Roll out a recipe of dough (amount used will depend on size and design of basket) to about ¼" to ½" thickness. Use the dough stiff so it will not stretch and tear as you work. Roll out two coils. Moisten lightly, then twist together, and place around the bowl rim. Cut remainder of dough into long strips about 1" to 1½" wide.

B. Begin to lay strips across the bowl and weave as shown, cutting off excess ends with scissors or knife. Moisten dough where the strips cross one another.

C. Use fork tines to adhere ends to twisted rim. Indent at overlaps with a decorative tool. Decorative balls may be placed on impressions. Smooth uneven areas and bake. Remove from oven and loosen carefully with knife blade if necessary.

D. With this method a flat rim results. It can be decorated by adding dough and rebaking or by gluing on decorations.

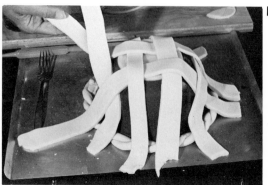

B

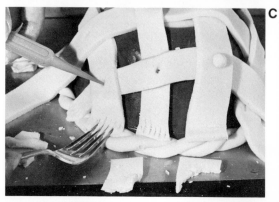

C

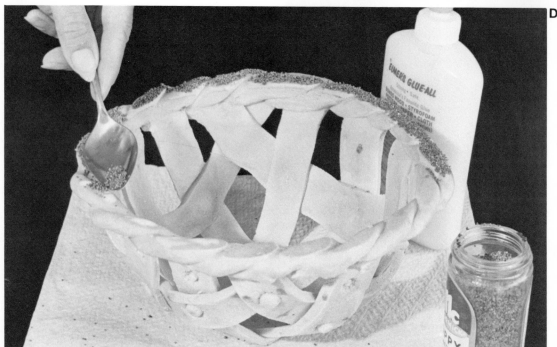

D

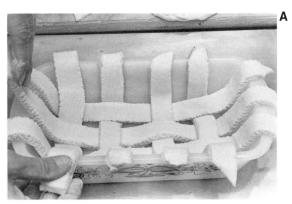

A

Method 2—Within the Form

A. The same principle is applied as above, but you lay the strips within the form and weave them, allowing each strip to overlap the edge.

B. Moisten the end of each strip and carefully place the rim around the top. Cut the excess strips and press against the bottom of the rim. Decorate the rim as desired. Observe that the strips in the top basket are smoothly cut; in this basket the strip edges were cut with a paring knife and resulted in a rougher, more textured look.

C. The finished basket with fruit decorations, hand painting, and satin glaze. By Dona Meilach.

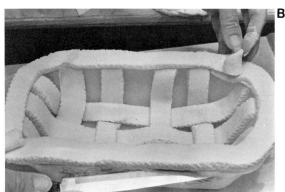

B

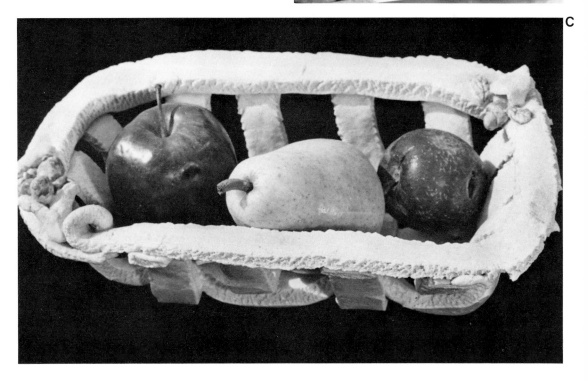

C

77

OTHER BASKETS

Designs cut out of cookie cutters are particularly well adapted to baskets. The only caution is to be sure all touching edges are well moistened and that more than one point of the designs touches another. If the attachment is not adequate, portions of the baked basket can detach and fall apart after the dough has cooled. The cookie-cutter procedure is demonstrated by Maureen Talbott: Examples are from her class.

A. Roll out and cut shapes with a cookie cutter.

B. Flower centers are made with a plastic dough tool.

C. Place each piece so it overlaps another on a well-greased metal baking pan.

D. Flowers and stars are combined.

E. Shapes have been cut with the edge of a small glass. A design was impressed on the panel or strip *before* placing it on the bowl. By Dona Meilach.

F. Shamrocks.

G. Hearts.

H. Twists; requires about 1½ recipes. By Beverly Stefansky.

I. Shamrocks and circles.

J. Top two baskets were made over a bowl. Bottom two were made inside a pie pan.

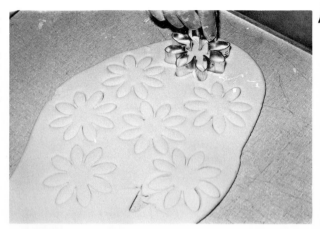

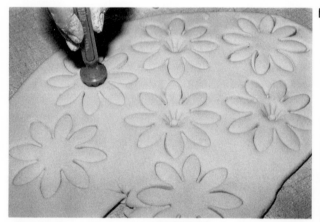

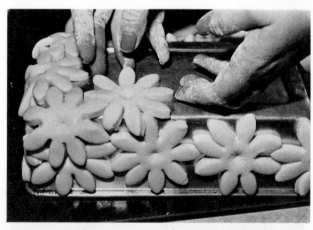

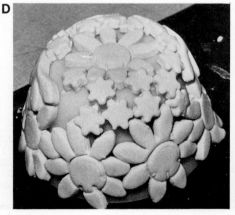

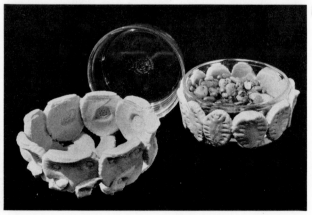

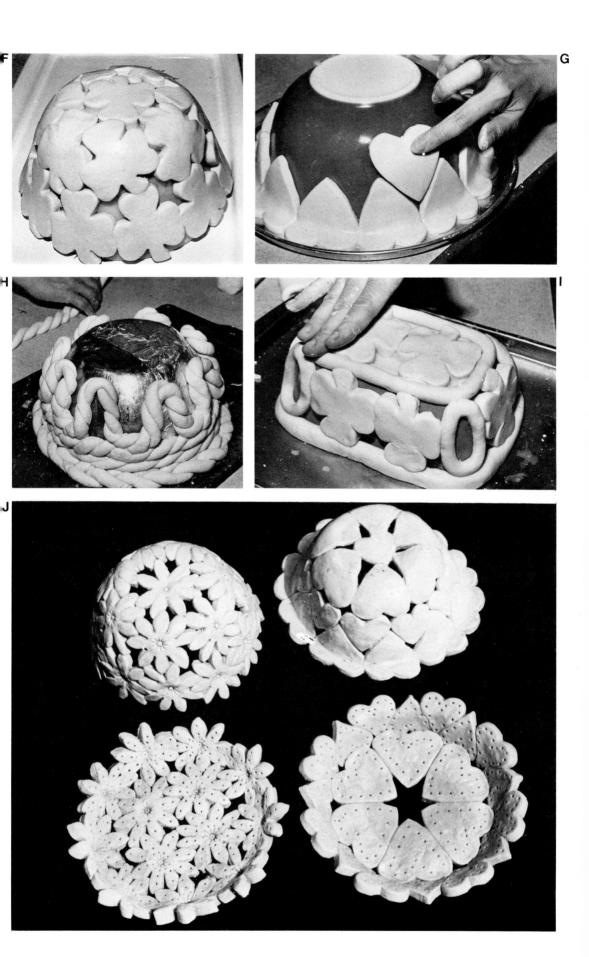

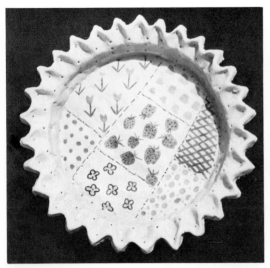

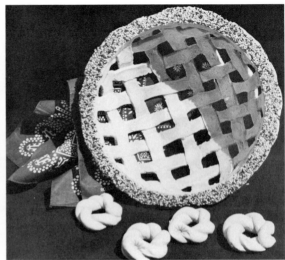

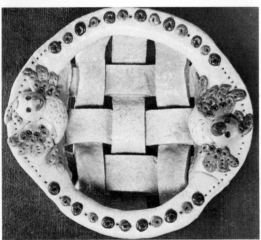

Top left: Patchwork basket by Maureen Talbott. Pan lined as a pie crust is decorated by hand painting.

Top right: By Maureen Talbott. Woven basket with birdseed glued to edge. Napkin rings are made from twisted lengths of dough.

Above and right: Two woven baskets by Kathie Fujisaka are fantastically decorated at the handles and around the rim. The baking form has protruding handles that support the shape.

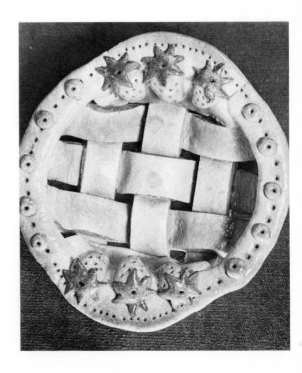

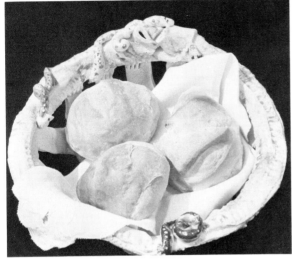

Left: Cleopatra basket. By Dona Meilach. A woven basket made within a Bundt cake pan has asps along the edges.

Below left: By Kay Whitcomb. Woven basket embellished with coils and balls.

Below: Woven rectangular basket by Maureen Talbott holds real bread and pretzel sticks that have been dried and preserved for display purposes by the method described below.

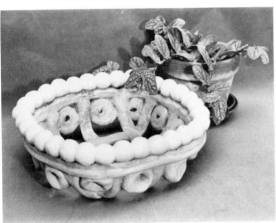

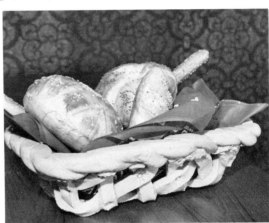

Drying and Finishing Real Bread for Display and for Sculptures

Many people like to have bread displayed in their baskets or to combine salt-dough objects with preserved real bread items. You can easily preserve any edible breads by the following process.

Bake or buy breadsticks, rolls, fancy or plain shaped bread in the bakery. You can use slices, French or Italian bread, bagels, Kaiser rolls, or whatever is available. Then

(a)   Dry the rolls thoroughly by placing them in a gas oven overnight so the pilot light does the drying, or in an electric oven for several hours at warm temperatures, or outdoors in the sun (protected by cheesecloth so the flies do not get to them) until dry and crispy.

(b)   Spray all surfaces with a household disinfectant such as Lysol so no bugs will find a home in the bread. Let dry thoroughly.

(c)   Coat with varnish brushed on generously but not puddled in the cracks and crevices of the bread. Use three or more coats, allowing to dry thoroughly between coats.

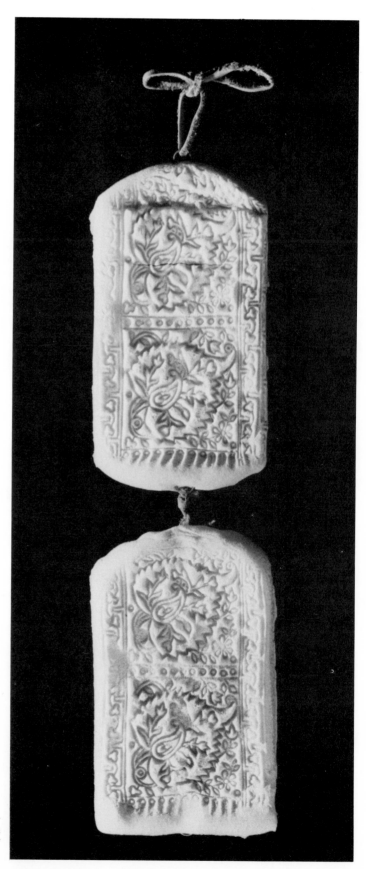

Double tableaux by Dona Meilach. Dough imprinted with a
wood printing block used for
printing fabrics in India.

7
IMPRINTS, MOLDS, CUTTERS

Imprints, molds, and precut shapes provide limitless possibilities to dough design. Imprinting can be accomplished with small tools and objects already shown, or you can use large predesigned blocks to make entire compositions. Portions of a block can be used, too, to change the direction of a motif or to imprint one on top of another slightly offset. Imprinted shapes can be cut apart, then reassembled, assemblage fashion, with other objects.

You will have to train your eye to discover objects that are applicable to imprinting. Generally, any design with a raised surface can be imprinted and leave its impression in the dough. Wood and linoleum printing blocks used for fabrics and for paper are excellent; the designs will always be reversed in the dough. Coins and medallions, highly embossed textiles that are woven and knotted also leave an impression. Use alphabets and numerals from children's printing sets or carved edges of wood trimming from lumber and handyman shops. Household items—glassware, sculpture, plaster plaques, wood carving—may have features you want impressed. If the piece is too big to place on the dough, try placing the dough against the object.

Dough to be imprinted should be stiff and dry. The imprint block should be floured, if necessary, or flour brushed on the dough's surface. Dough that is too soft and moist may stick to the block and not hold a raised edge. Too much moisture in the dough also causes puffiness and bubbling during baking, which can ruin the imprint.

Molds are forms into which the dough is pushed until it picks up the design of the form. They are excellent for reproducing shapes, yet each can be individualized by decorating differently. For people who question their own artistic abilities, a mold can be an excellent introduction to the creative potential of dough art. You will always get a reliable form from which you can expand your creative talents.

Cookie cutters can be used for duplicating shapes also. Despite the sameness of one mold, each can be treated differently; try adding more dough onto parts, adding details, changing color combinations and interior design. Add one form onto another; add cut forms onto backings and plaques. Cutters are sold for cookies, gingerbread people, holiday motifs, for canapés, ceramics, and candies. You can fashion your own from metal strapping tape available from large hardware dealers.

Imprinted and cut forms can be applied for unending decorative purposes; for duplicating designs in wallpapers and fabrics as plaques to be hung on walls, for making beads, jewelry, and any repeat design motifs.

Use all the techniques throughout the book and combine with one another. For example, several baskets are made with cookie-cut shapes. The wreaths (chapter 10) employ canapé-cut shapes to build up the design. Also, cut with edges of glasses, make large circles with bowls, heart-shape pans, ovals with serving dishes, scalloped edges with the glass top from a lantern. Look around. Use anything that will work for the design you want.

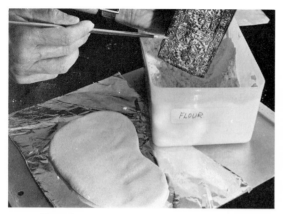

To make an imprint, have the dough stiff and dry so it holds up the edges of the fine design. Dust the block with flour or cornstarch and shake off excess.

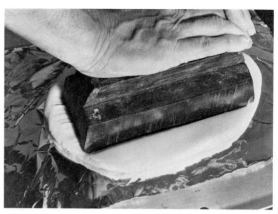

Roll out the dough to desired thickness, and press the design into the dough very hard without sliding it in any direction.

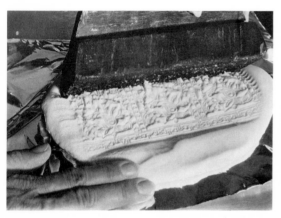

Lift block carefully; if any dough adheres to block, it is best to reknead, reroll the dough, redust the block, and begin again.

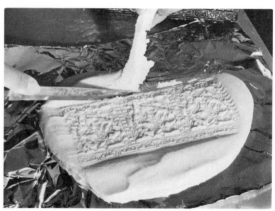

Cut around the edges of the design.

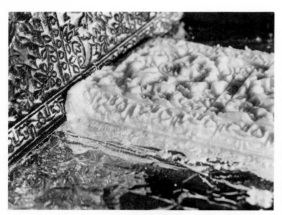

Use the edge of the block to carry the imprint around the edge of the dough. Be careful not to push so hard that the original block is misshaped.

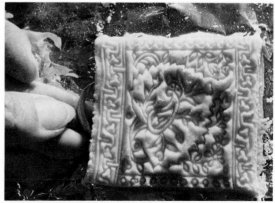

Portions of the imprint can be cut and used for pendants. Be sure to add a hanging device; in this one a pop-top lid pull is embedded.

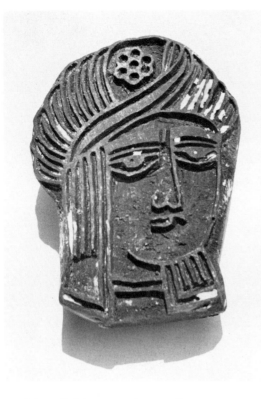
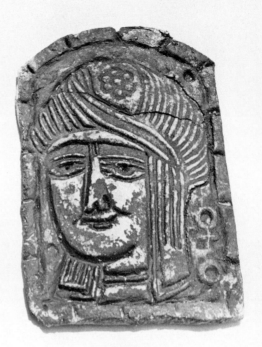

Arlene Seitzinger used an antique newspaper printer's cut to make the imprinted design at right. Then she used portions of the cut to make the shardlike blocks around the unusual panel below entitled "Coffee Gossip (Circa ?)." 18" high, 18" wide. The panel, with beautifully sculptured relief designs and an antique finish, resembles a priceless relic from an ancient civilization.

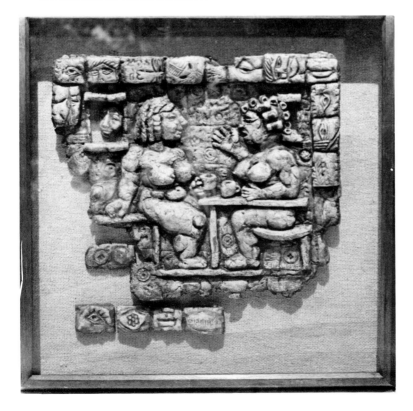

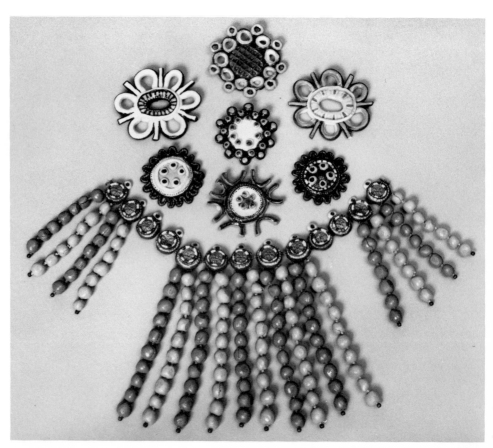

Many kinds of beads and jewelry can be made with bread dough. *Above*, Gretchen McCarthy's choker and pins are beautifully crafted. Infinite designs can be made by imprinting a variety of buttons and other forms into the dough. For fine stringing holes, embed a length of hollow #5 raw spaghetti within the bead, and use nylon fishing line for string. *At right*, pins are made with circles and coils and the centers imprinted with buttons. *(Courtesy, Illinois Bronze Paint Co., Lake Zurich, Illinois)*

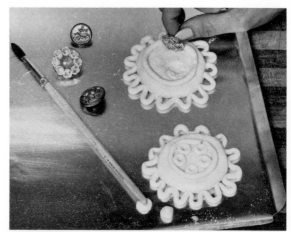

Large round beads can be made over paper straws, greased food skewers, or metal knitting needles, and suspended over pan edges for baking. If a bead is laid flat on a pan, one side will be flat. A medallion can be made for lacing onto macramé or weavings by spanning a straw with strips of dough. When the straw is removed, it will allow a cord to be laced through and the medallion will hang flat against the backing.

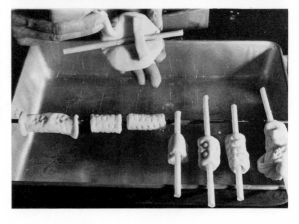

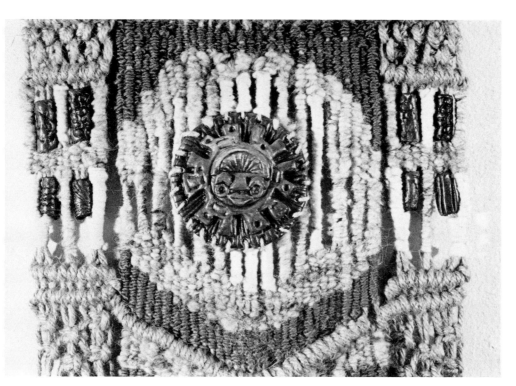

Medallions and beads of imprinted bread dough are shown in this closeup detail of the large macramé plant hanger at right. By Rosemary Fee. The deftly antiqued and highly glazed finish has the appearance of ceramics.

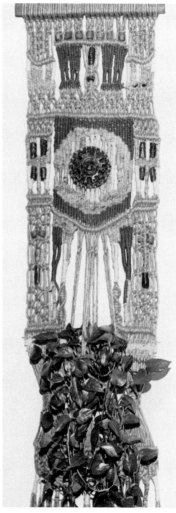

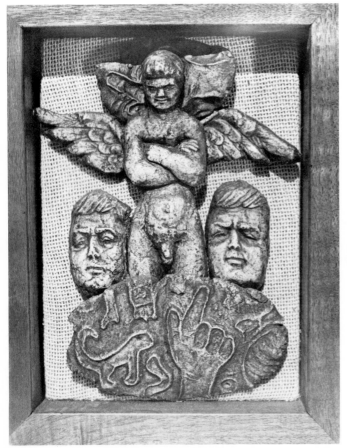

"Man and His Universe." By Arlene Seitzinger. Created from assembled impressions.

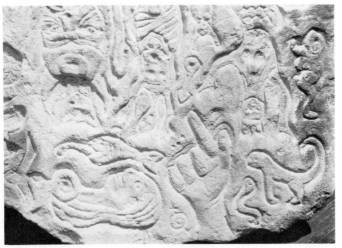

Detail of "Man and His Universe," created by using a variety of stamped impressions on one piece of dough.

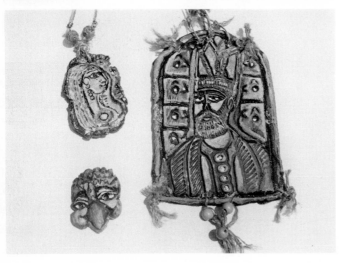

Jewelry by Arlene Seitzinger made from imprinted forms.

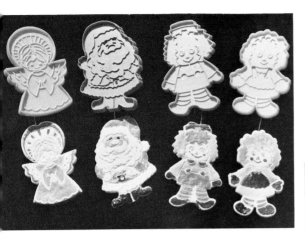

COOKIE-CUT FIGURES

Maureen Talbott creates a variety of Christmas ornaments with cookie cutters already shaped with inner details, available from Hallmark dealers and craft shops.

An aluminum cookie cutter gives only the outline of the figure. You can paint the flat design or place additional bread-dough shapes on top of it. You can also create your own cutters by shaping metal strapping tape (from hardware stores): a perfect idea for those who want to make original designs and then mass-produce them.

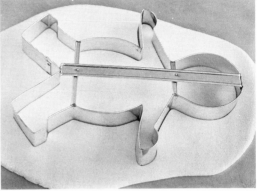

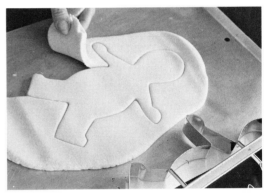

Shannon Yewell's simple cookie-cutter designs are intricately and individually painted and backed with a pin clasp for jewelry.

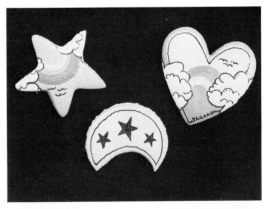

Susan Lyon Petelik uses bright felt-tip markers to decorate ornaments made from animal-shaped cookie cutters. (Courtesy, artist)

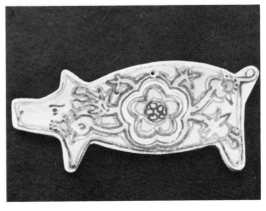

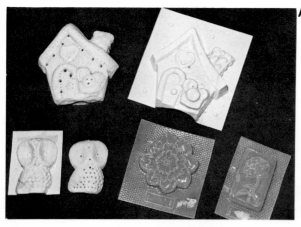

SHAPES FROM MOLDS

There is a wide variety of shaped molds available in metals and plastics that are adaptable to bread-dough creations. Look for bread, cake, and candy molds in cake-decorating catalogs and in the housewares sections of department stores. At your craft shop you will find plastic and metal molds used for making plastercrafts and candles. You can improvise molds from found objects, but be sure there are no deep undercuts that would prevent the form from separating from the mold.

A. Plastic craft molds interpreted in bread dough.

B. Maureen Talbott demonstrates the use of a flower mold; cornstarch or flour is brushed lightly into the mold. Use stiff dough; wad into a smooth ball. . .

C. . . . press solidly into mold. Dough should be kneaded well to eliminate as many air bubbles as possible.

D. Carefully separate dough from mold and lift out.

E. Before baking, poke several holes into top of mold with toothpick to release any trapped air and prevent dough from bubbling and/or rising during baking, a fault that frequently occurs with thick pieces of compressed dough. Holes can be made in unobtrusive areas of the design or made obviously as part of the design.

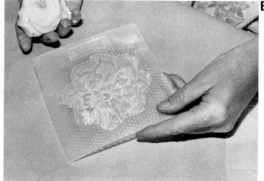

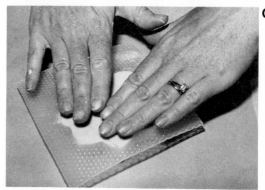

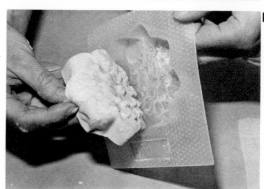

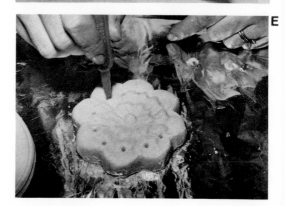

90

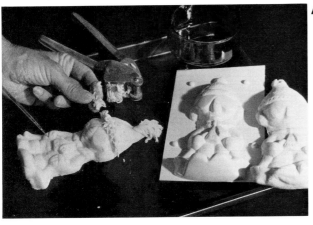

A

A. The front half only of a plastic two-part mold is used to create a baseball player. After the figure is pulled from the mold, it can be individualized by adding fringe for the hat and scarf ends.

B. Figure molds usually have thin and thick portions that require the dough to be pressed in carefully to fill up all areas.

C. The thicker parts can be thinned by scooping some of the dough out from the back. It is possible to place dough in the back half of the mold. When both halves have been baked, add a strip of dough around both pieces to make a three-dimensional standing figure. After baking, if the base is not flat, it can be straightened on a belt sander used for woodworking.

D. Another efficient way to separate the dough from the mold is to place a single layer from a sheet of facial tissue into the mold; then place the dough in the mold. Remove by pulling up on the tissue.

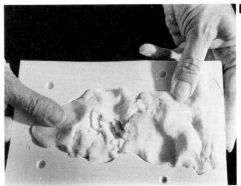

B

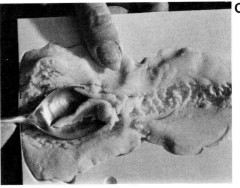

C

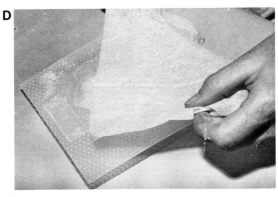

D

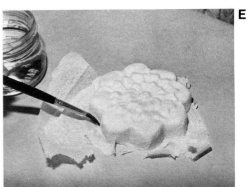

E

E. and F. Then moisten the edge of the tissue and pull away the excess, leaving the layer of tissue on the design. Bake with tissue on and paint; it bakes into the mold and keeps the design firm.

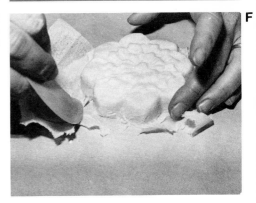

F

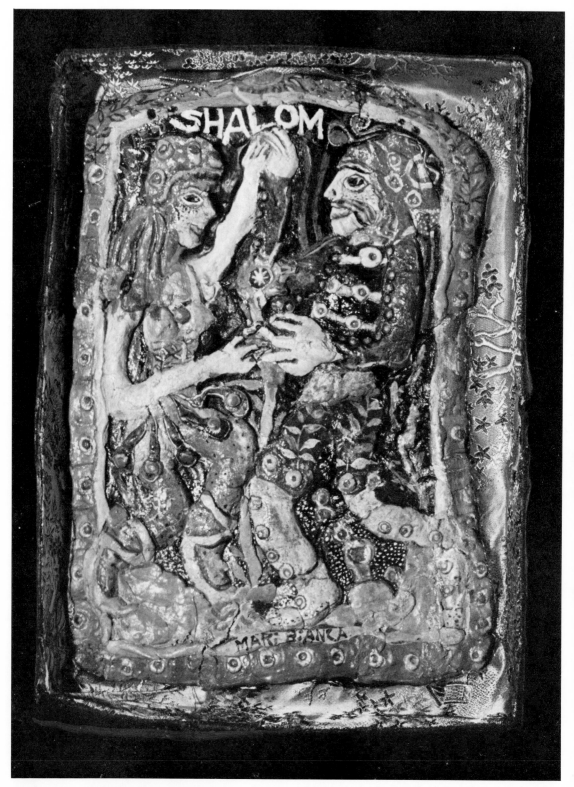

"Shalom." By Mari Bianca. 8″ by 10″ bread-dough forms plaque mounted on wood.

8
PLAQUES AND OTHER PRESENTATIONS

Many bread-dough sculptures are displayed advantageously and attractively on backings or within frames that give them added dimension and importance. When you create your sculptures, you should plan the presentation for you may have to incorporate mounting devices before you bake the object.

The wood plaque, treated in many ways, is a popular presentation method. Pieces of old weathered wood used in their natural finish (cleaned, of course) can be scrounged from old building sites, dumps, neighbors' throwaways, and garage sales. New pieces of backing wood that you can paint, stain, antique, and varnish are available in craft shops where decoupage supplies are sold. Your local lumberyard or friendly woodworker may have scraps that are perfect, too. Use pine and stain in many shades, or use exotic woods such as teak, ebony, mahogany, and then oil and varnish to bring out the natural grains. A small router can yield a beveled or other decorative edge. Edges and surfaces can be given textural treatments by singeing with a propane torch and going over the burned areas with a wire brush.

Branches, twigs, and driftwood found at the beach and forest preserves make excellent backings and stands for some pieces. Remember to bake found wood objects for an hour or so at low temperatures to destroy any fungi. They may be sprayed with a household disinfectant and dried thoroughly.

Simple and ornate frames are a popular treatment for sculptures. Old frames can be culled from used furniture dealers, junkyards, and yard sales. New frames are available from art-craft suppliers and discount and department stores. Try plastic mounts, cork panels alone or on white wood, natural wood on finished wood, and any combination. Try filling the compartments of ecology boxes, too.

Many subjects can be enhanced by adding dried weed and flowers glued around the base of the figure. You can pick dried weeds in season, dry some yourself, or buy them from floral and gift shops. Spray dried weeds with hair spray to prevent them from deterioration.

Adhere bread-dough objects to backing with white glue, household cements, or epoxies, depending upon the composition of the backing. Large heavy figures should also have a securing device such as a wire or hook baked into them. These can be attached to nails in the mounting board and combined with glue.

Panel backgrounds may also be made of decorative wallpapers or shelf papers, felt, burlap, and other compatible materials glued onto a wood or Masonite backing. The covering should be glued and brought around to the back of the panel so the edges are covered also. Thin wood slats could be nailed to the edges to serve as a frame; a wider slat will give the impression of a shadow box.

Often a backing will inspire a bread-dough creation. Printer's font drawers have rectangular and diagonal dividers that create spaces for interestingly shaped figures. Use old furniture drawers, jewelry boxes, cigar boxes, and so forth.

Study the examples throughout the book to observe the infinite ways bread-dough creations can be attractively displayed and presented.

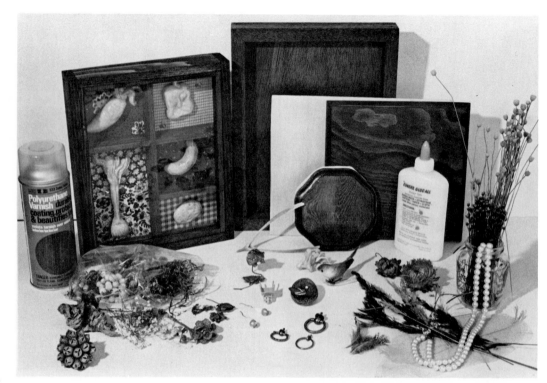

Materials for mounting bread-dough figures and embellishing them include: wood panels, dried flowers, glue, small ready-made objects or some you create yourself from Recipe No. 2 (bread and glue), jewelry and decorative hangers. The ecology box, lined with different fabrics with sculptures in each space, is by Maureen Talbott.

A group of children made this plaque over a piece of chicken wire nailed to a piece of fiberboard. Precolored doughs were stretched onto the chicken wire, which forms an excellent support ground for the dough. Blue is used for the sky, green for the ground. (*Courtesy, Barbara Herberholz*)

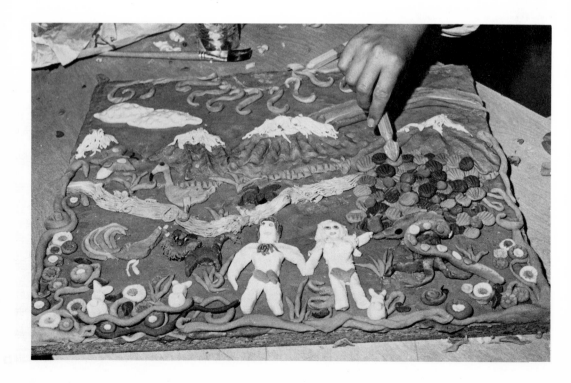

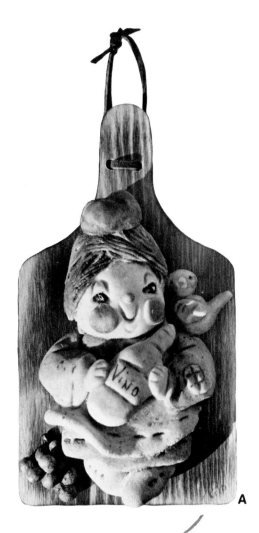

A

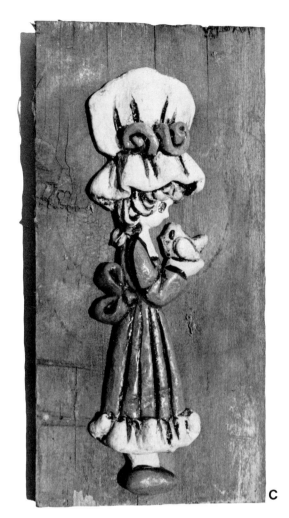

C

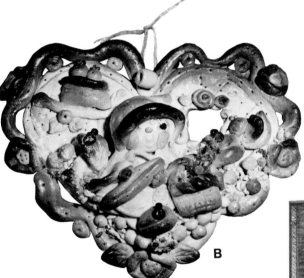

B

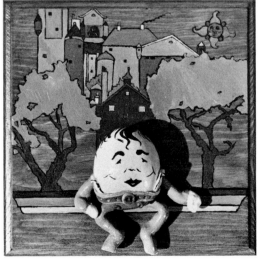

D

A. By Rita Martinez de Blake (Mama's Cookie Factory). The figure is mounted on a breadboard.

B. By Rita Martinez de Blake. The bread dough itself is the backing for the heart-shape relief sculpture.

C. By Rosemary Fee. The antique finish on the figure blends in well with the natural panel of found weathered wood.

D. Humpty Dumpty, by Maureen Talbott, sits on a fence that has been painted directly on mahogany with acrylic paints. Board and figure are sealed with varnish.

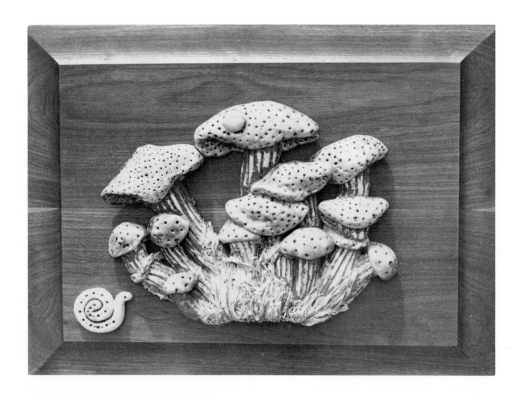

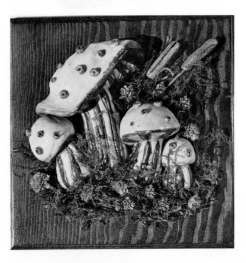

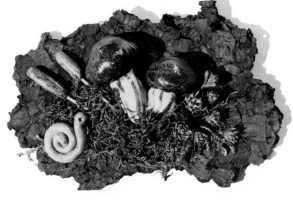

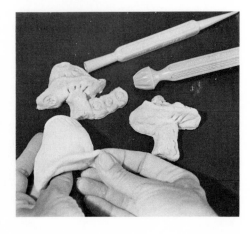

Three mushroom plaques by Maureen Talbott. The bottom plaques use dried flowers and miniature items glued over the dough. Stripes on stems are made by brushing wood stain on with a cotton tip. Ideas for mushroom shapes can be found in botanical and garden books and cookbooks with mushroom varieties.

Mushroom shapes can be easily created over thumbs and fingers. Very rounded ones can be placed over mounds of aluminum foil.

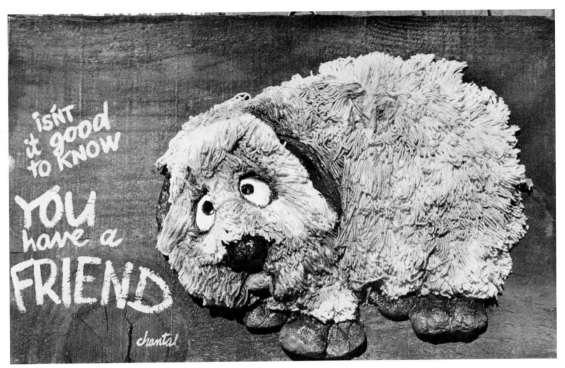

Above: Shaggy dog on a delightful plaque by Chantal uses lengths and lengths of bread dough put through a garlic press.

Right: Carrots, on a cork backing, are made with the same type of strands as the dog's hair. Carrots may be shaped over the fingers as are the mushrooms. By Maureen Talbott.

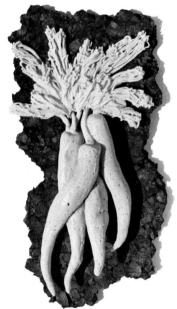

Lumps of dough are put into the cup of a garlic press and the handle squeezed. As long as you continue to feed dough into the cup and do not cut the strands they will get longer and longer. When the strands reach the desired length, place them near the figure. Cut and lay in position Always adhere sections with water. Wetter dough will result in finer strands than stiff dough.

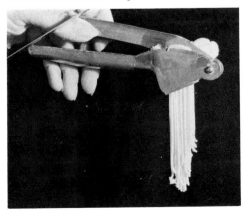
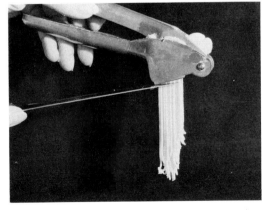

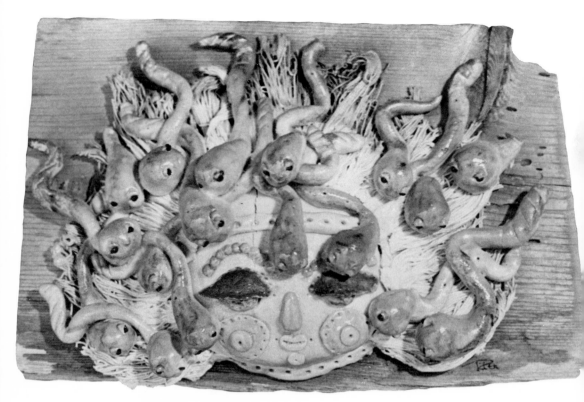

"Maddusa" by Rita Martinez de Blake. Head was
formed over a ball of foil, hair added, then facial features and snakes made from balls and coils. Twenty
coats of varnish, front and back, were used.

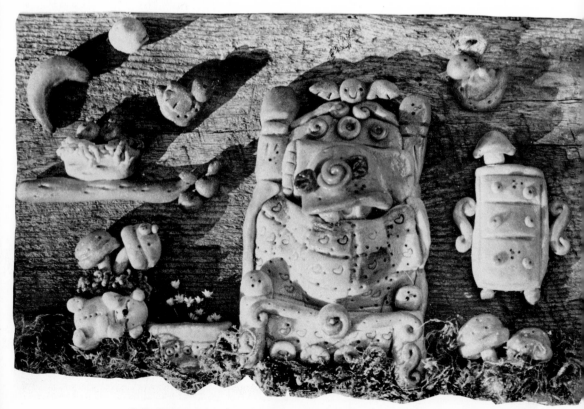

Potbellied stove plaque consists of separate bread-
dough pieces and dried flowers assembled onto the
backing. By Rita Martinez de Blake.

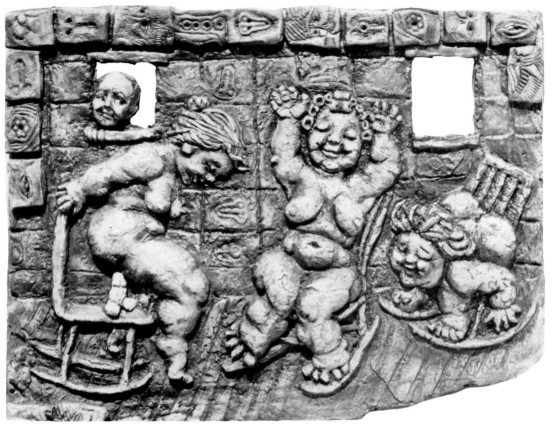

"Rocking Frolic." By Arlene Seitzinger. The modeled and imprinted shapes were made on a piece of pegboard so the dough would work through the holes and be held in place. The pegboard was cut where the windows appear.

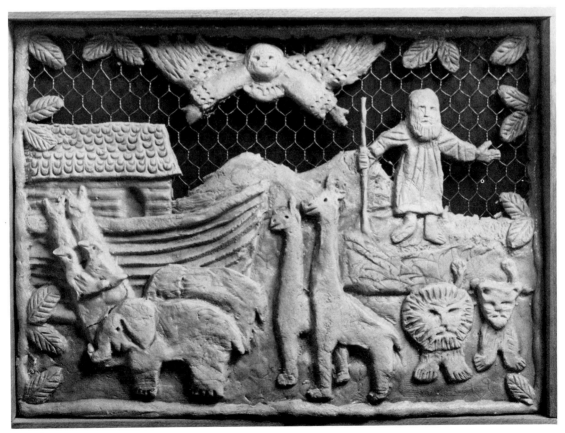

"Noah's Ark." By Hattie Waddell. Chicken wire set in a frame over a wood backing supports the bread-dough forms. (Courtesy, artist)

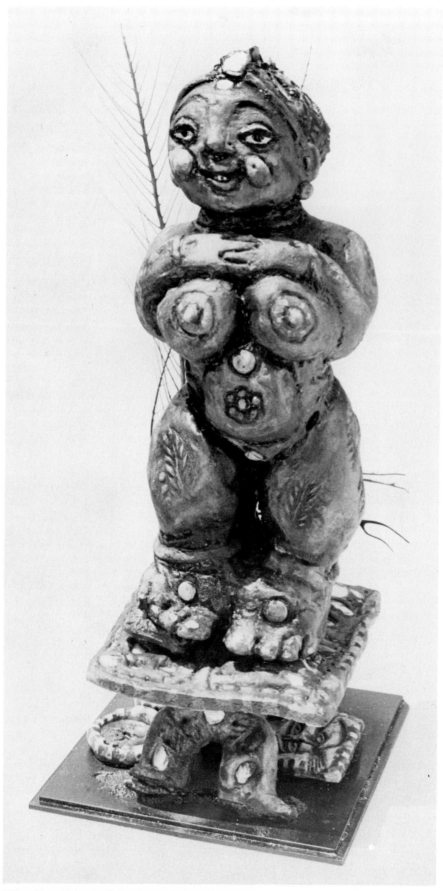

"Mrs. Circa Unknown." By Arlene Seitzinger. Bread
dough used very moist, as clay, is applied over a form
made of rigid polyurethane. Urethane, as opposed to
polyfoam-Styrofoam, does not melt when baked at
260°. The armature remains in the form.

9

SCULPTURE-WORKING IN THREE DIMENSIONS

All bread-dough sculptures have dimensions because of the nature of the material. Most are flat on the back, allowing them to be hung on a wall or on a plaque. Creating a totally three-dimensional form that is designed for viewing as is a wood, stone, or metal sculpture requires some challenging procedures that are fun and well worth the effort.

Bread dough has not enjoyed status as an art medium in the same category as the traditional materials of bronze, wood, marble, and clay. It has remained outside the milieu of the serious sculptor. The bronze fountain created by Ruth Asawa (chapter 1) is a step forward in this adaptation to serious sculpture, but still the dough itself was not used for the final form. Therefore, at the inception of the idea for this book, the problem was put to several people who normally worked in other media, and the results can be seen on the following pages.

Arlene Seitzinger, an Indiana sculptor, known for her versatility in sculpture media, had no familiarity with the usual application of bread dough. Given only the recipe and how to bake it, she began to apply the dough over armatures and over previously used scrap materials that would be compatible to the medium, and she baked these upright in her oven. The result was the figure shown at left. It belies its materials because of the shaping, presentation, and finish. You have to be told it is made of dough before you would believe, by touch or sight, that it is not wood or patinaed metal.

Arlene approached bread dough in the same way she uses clay: to create a form by modeling, pinching, adding to, and carving away. Then she realized that if the dough was applied soft and moist over an existing form made of rigid polyurethane that would not deteriorate under low oven temperatures, any shape could be accomplished. The principle is similar to working over foil but the rigid polyurethane is sturdier and more reliable for heavy, upright figures.

Another excellent base for three-dimensional pieces is a can, and this is shown in the examples by Kay Whitcomb. Several cans can be wired together and covered with foil to make a large shape (see color section, the pig centerpiece), then covered with bread dough and decorated.

Another approach is the assembled form created by adding one shape onto another by placement, by gluing, or by double baking. For example, a shape could be formed around a bowl; then a cylindrical shape made over a can, or other object could be added. Rita Martinez de Blake made a series of mouse houses by adding a flat bottom and top to a cylindrical center.

You can also achieve three dimensionality by baking five flat pieces and combining them in a square with a top, or by simply covering a box with dough for a square presentation.

An imaginative approach to the sculptural form has been easily and delightfully solved by Julia Marshall's muffin cup series. Julia, too, had never seen bread dough made into anything other than baskets when she found the recipe and began working. The results are highly individualized.

Small sculptures can be made over shaped foil, but you must begin to think of three-dimensional, upright objects as opposed to flat-backed figures. Think, too, of other ways to support them using any means you can—any kinds of props in the oven, any kinds of combinations. The examples on the following pages should help stimulate your thinking.

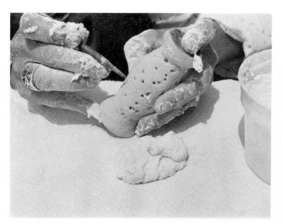
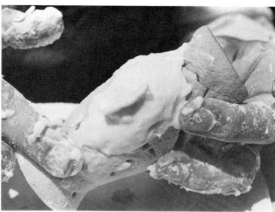

The process of building up a sculpture such as the one shown on page 100 is demonstrated by Arlene Seitzinger. A shape of rigid urethane is pierced with a toothpick to allow air and heat to penetrate.

Bread dough mixed very moist is applied over the urethane until the desired shape is achieved. It is then modeled in the same fashion as clay and baked. In this way completely three-dimensional sculptures can be created. Size is limited only by the oven that is used, although experimentation can result in two-part baking procedures or in gluing one shape to another for larger pieces. Commercial ovens can be employed also.

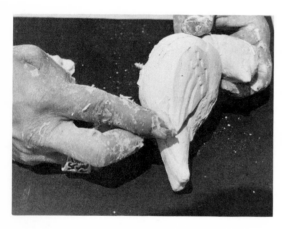

Arlene demonstrates how the dough can also be molded over any bakable object such as this plaster bird. A variety of plaster forms can be obtained in ceramic shops, and they can be used for digressions into other sculptural compositions. It would be pointless to follow the exact contours and duplicate such an item in bread dough.

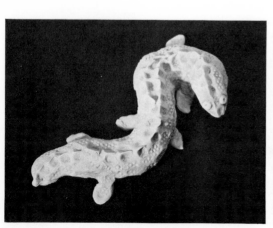

Three-dimensional pieces can also be formed over foil shapes, as in this dragon by Mimi Levinson.

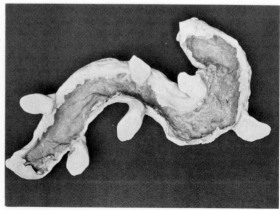

The underside shows the construction. The possibilities are infinite.

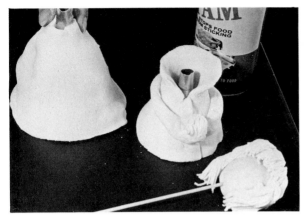 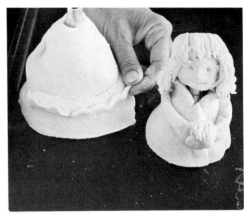

Three-dimensional forms can be constructed from several pieces. Two different size funnels form the skirt and torso for a figure. The head is shaped around a foil ball and placed on a long skewer. The funnels must be well greased with cooking oil so they will separate from the dough after baking. The

head can be placed on the smaller funnel end for baking and held upright by the skewer. After baking, the funnels are removed; a circle of unbaked dough can be used around the waist of the skirt, the torso placed over it and rebaked for final assembly. Or the top can be glued to the bottom.

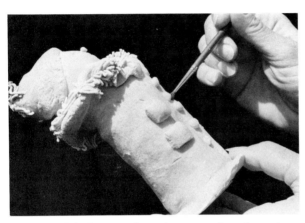 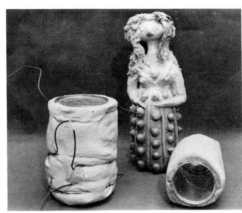

This figure was formed over a cardboard cone from inside a ball of twine. The cone is extremely hard and will not burn at low temperatures: it remains within the piece permanently.

Kay Whitcomb bakes three-dimensional figures over frozen juice cans. Wire embedded within the dough during baking is used to help strengthen the figure and support the upper torso. She may bake one layer or one portion, then add on parts in subsequent bakings.

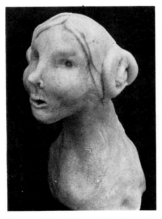 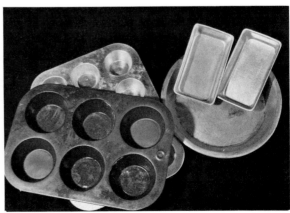

A modeled head in bread dough can be made over a small frozen juice can for the neck and shoulders and aluminum foil for the head. By Lynda Bauer.

Deep muffin tins and small baking pans can also be used for creating three-dimensional sculptures as shown in the examples by Julia Marshall on the following page.

103

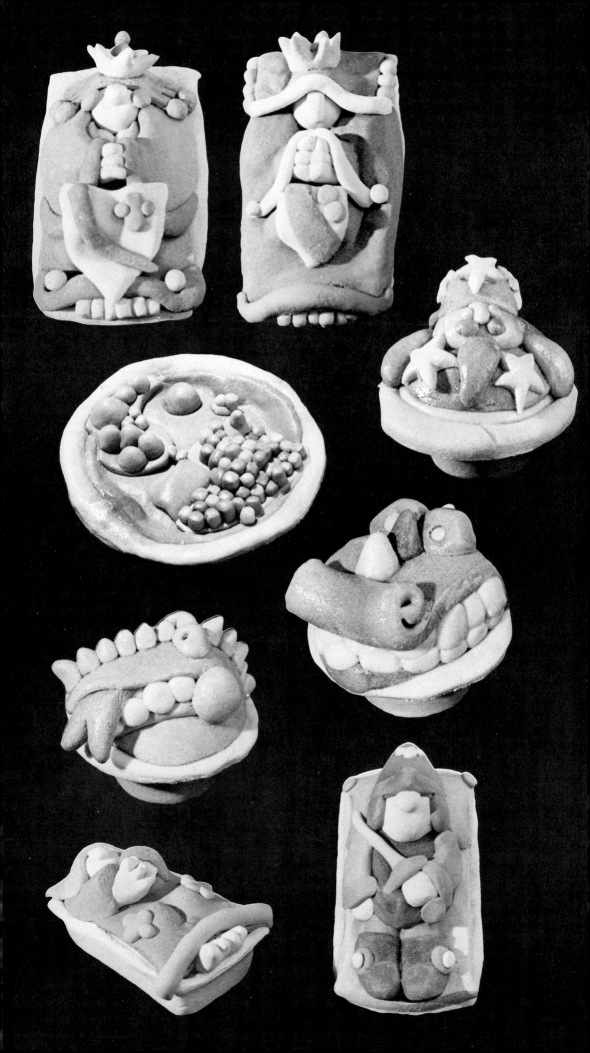

Opposite: A wildly inspired assortment of sculptural objects have been created by Julia Marshall by baking in muffin and pie tins and small baking pans (see previous page). They include (*from top to bottom*) a king and queen; a pie plate in the form of a topographical map of San Francisco; an officer of the law. Next are her "monster muffins" and a monk and knight from the "sarcophagus family," which includes the king and queen above. All are made by coloring the raw dough with watercolors, then baking and glazing with Varathane varnish.

Right, top: Rita Martinez de Blake works her favorite subjects within a pan, thereby creating a high sculptural relief form. *Below:* By Rita Martinez de Blake. Cans wrapped with foil could be used for shapes such as this fantasy animal in three dimensions. (*Photographed at the Marco Polo Shop, Santa Fe, New Mexico*)

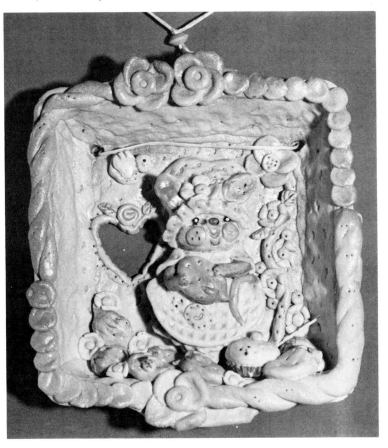

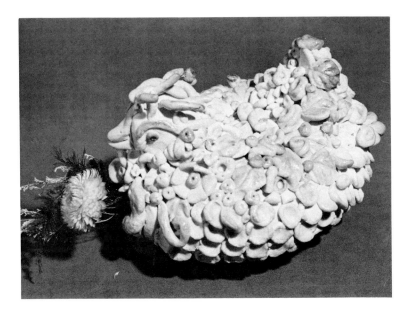

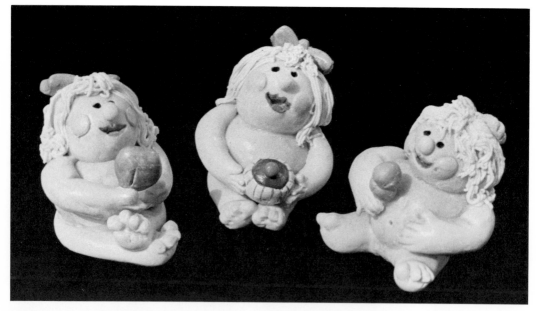

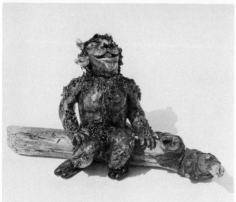

"Weight Watchers." By Pat Smiley. Each figure, molded over aluminum foil, is 2½" high.

"Demon" by Pat Smiley is 6" high, 9" wide, and 3" deep. He is made over foil also, and is perched on a twig.

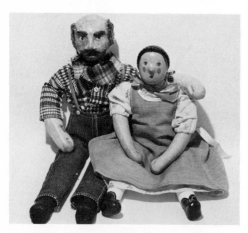

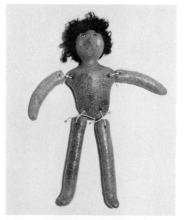

The farmer and his wife dolls by Paul and Sue Krosnick have hinged bread-dough bodies with fabric clothes. They can be dressed and undressed. The undressed body of a doll, *at right,* shows the understructure. A complete family could be created, or one could make an ethnic doll collection.

Bread dough is used for heads only and sometimes for hands in the fabric-clothed dolls by Carolyn Schmitz.

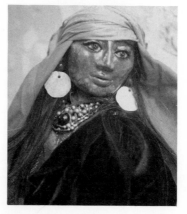

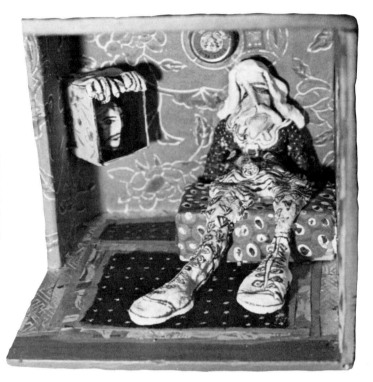

Box environments by Mari Bianca use bread-dough figures and heads and objects that are scaled down to the size of the composition desired. Objects hang on walls, sit within boxes, and are placed on the floors of the room settings that range from cigar-box size to wooden crate.

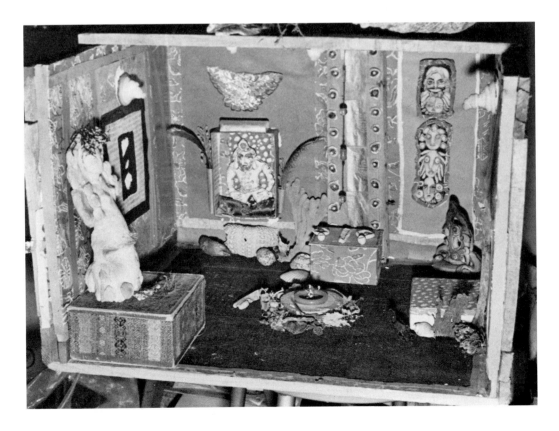

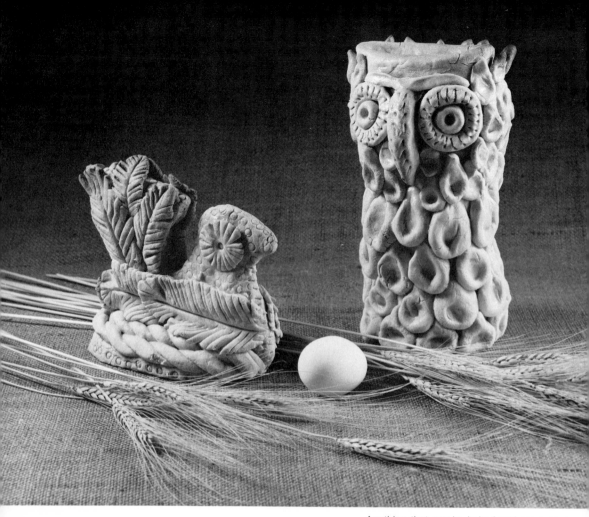

Anything that can be baked and serve as a form can be used, as shown in Edna Kuhta's three-dimensional objects: a rooster formed over cans and foil and an owl formed over a large juice can. *Opposite page,* the figures, vases, and a box are easily developed with imagination and engineering.

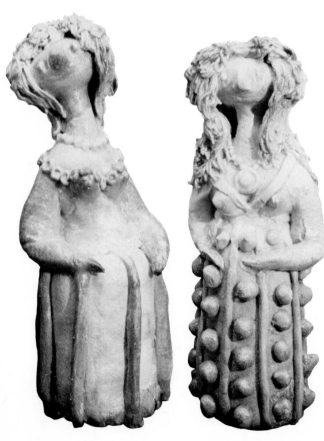

Kay Whitcomb builds two girls over juice cans in which wires have been embedded for extra strength and to prevent the dough from shrinking.

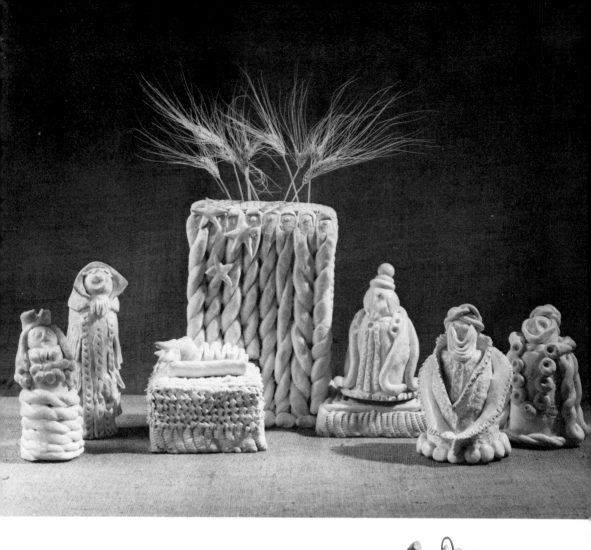

"Man Does Not Live By Bread Alone" by Kay Whitcomb. The opposite side repeats the exterior design, but has a mirror embedded. One side was baked flat, then the piece was turned over and the opposite side developed on top and rebaked. The mounting dowel was added during the baking. After painting and glazing, the sculpture was mounted on the wooden block.

Candelabrum by Gretchen McCarthy is made of wooden dowels with bread-dough ornaments suspended and perched on short, narrow dowels. Rings with bread-dough droplets also surround the uprights where the horizontal rods connect. Dowels are drilled to accept the crossing rods. Candleholders are placed at ends. Ornaments are painted in fluorescent colors so they glow in the dark. (Courtesy, Illinois Bronze Paint Co., Lake Zurich, Illinois)

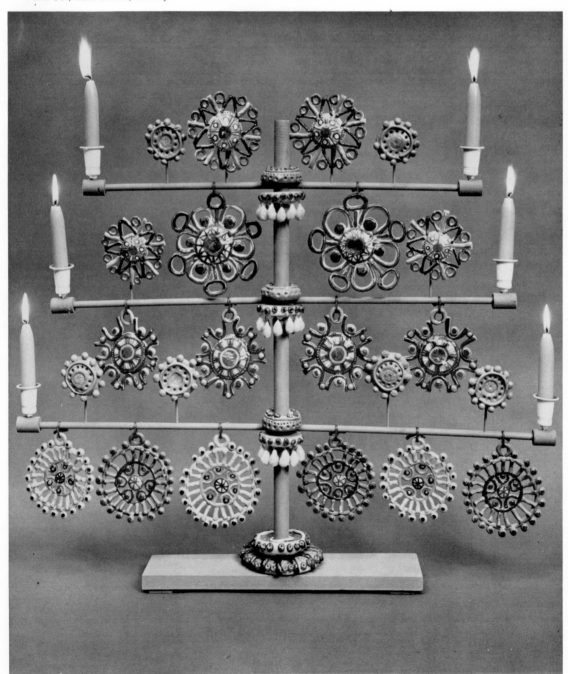

10
HOLIDAY IDEAS

Edible cookie dough has been traditionally used for Christmas ornaments, and the aroma of gingerbread and butter cookies baking before the holidays conjures nostalgia. But in this day of bakeries, frozen foods, and never enough time to do all the things we would like, the practice of making permanent ornaments that can be used year in and year out is gaining popularity. Nothing could be more fun than re-creating some of your favorite shapes and decorating them so they can be admired and remembered every year. They make excellent gifts, too.

No matter what the season, you can think "holidays" by creating batches of objects ahead of time, or using leftovers from other projects to make a few items for any special occasion. Some ornament ideas are shown in earlier chapters, but the following examples can spark additional ideas.

Cookie cutters in a variety of Christmas and geometric shapes such as trees, stars, diamonds, Santa Claus, snowmen, reindeer, and so forth are easy to find. Make ornaments also with circles and coils, with free-form shapes cut from rolled dough and decorated with beads and sequins.

You can save hours of painting time by using precolored dough and different colored flour. Whole-wheat flour glazed with egg makes the most natural colored gingerbread doll you would ever hope to find. Add whole cloves or other hard-shaped spices for eyes, real buttons or white dough down the chest.

Colored bits of the bread and glue recipe can be added to the salt dough during baking. Also embed colored objects in the dough such as beads, glass, colored glittery crystalline beads used in decorating costumes, gold and silver metallic ribbons, tiny findings such as miniature toys, dolls, baskets, and so forth. Just be sure they will not melt. Sometimes thinner plastic items will curl at the edges and give exactly the effect you want for wreaths. Always pretest to make sure the objects will hold up during baking.

Create sculptural dough objects to include in dried flower arrangements and centerpieces at Easter, Thanksgiving, Valentine's Day, for bridal and baby showers, and as place-card holders for every occasion. Remember to try wild colorings, too, such as fluorescent paints, silver, golds, pewters, and other metallic finishes.

Bright flowers and sprigs of jewelry made of delicately formed glue dough can be attached to jewelry findings and used for pins, rings, and earrings depicting holiday ideas at any season.

Christmas ornaments using the crushed candy technique, page 60, can be used for see-through colorful ornaments and a stained-glass window effect in church and building panels.

Of course, if the temptation to make edible ornaments is irresistible, the same techniques and many of the designs shown throughout the book can be applied to your own favorite cookie and bread recipes.

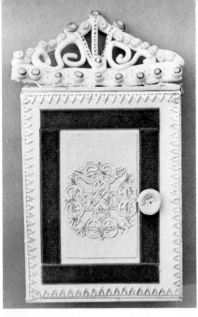
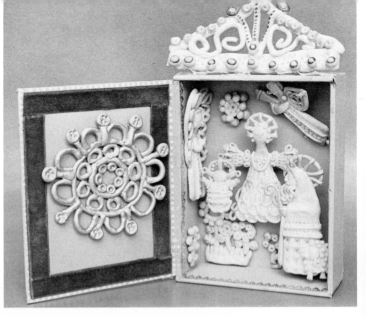

Crèche in a box. By Gretchen McCarthy. Closed and open views. The box is colorfully decorated with velvet ribbons, paper, and fabrics. A bread-dough knob and top ornament set the stage for the magnificently crafted figures within. *(Courtesy, Illinois Bronze Paint Co., Lake Zurich, Illinois)*

A crèche by Kay Whitcomb with the Three Wise Men.

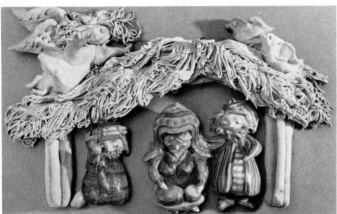

Another crèche by Kay Whitcomb.

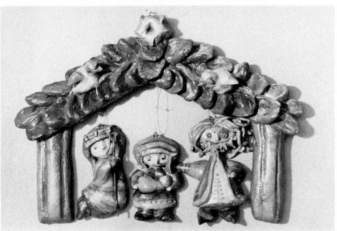

Noel plaque by Gracie Kramer.

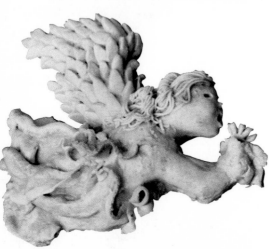

Angel by Lynda Bauer.

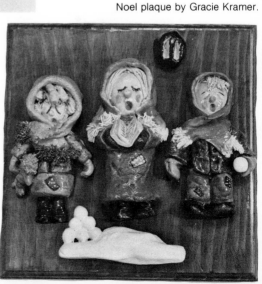

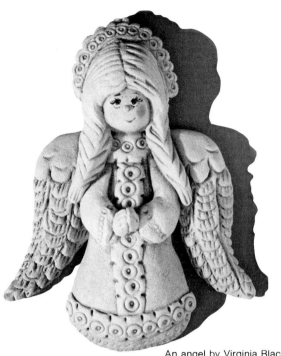

An angel by Virginia Black.

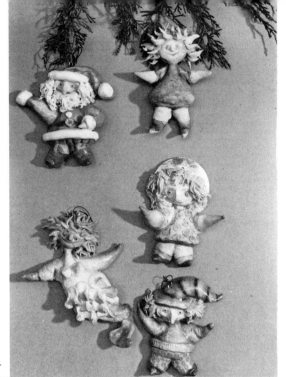

Ornaments for the tree by Kay Whitcomb.

Reindeer and rider by Kay Whitcomb.

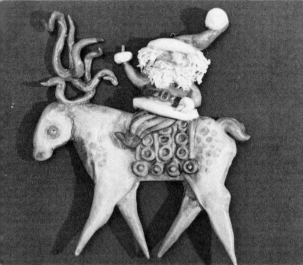

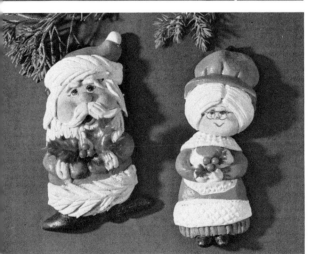

Mr. and Mrs. Santa Claus by Virginia Black.

Cherubs and birds by Pat Smiley.

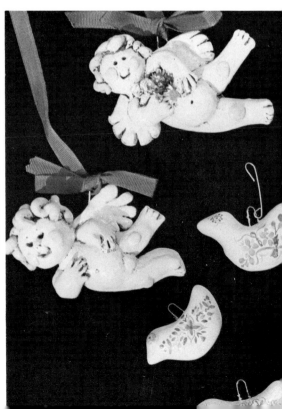

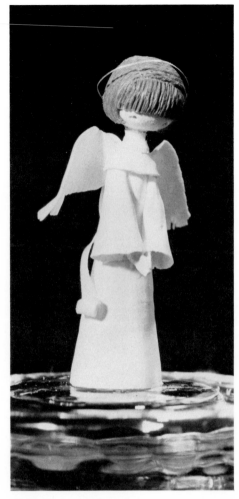

Angel. By Linda Fugate. 2″ high. Made of bread and glue dough.

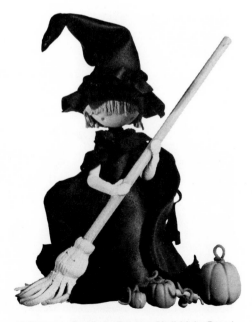

Halloween. By Linda Fugate. 2½″ high. Bread and glue dough.

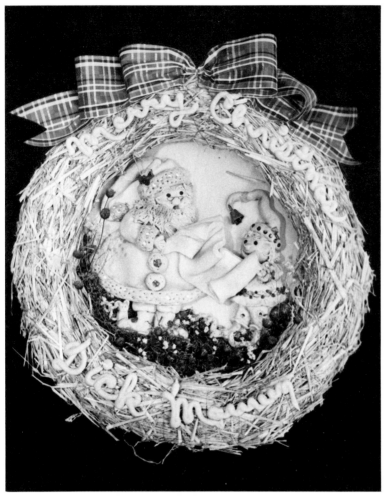

Wreath. By Maureen Talbott. About 15" diameter. Straw wreath from a craft shop is backed with wood and baker's clay sculptures laid within. Pieces are made by two bakings. Lettering is written with a cake decorator.

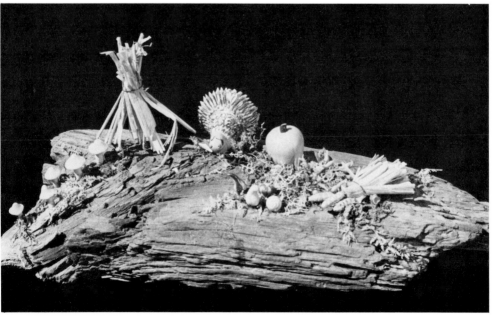

Thanksgiving centerpiece. By Bernice A. Houston. Bread and glue dough objects placed on a branch with straw, dried flowers, and moss. 3½" high.

115

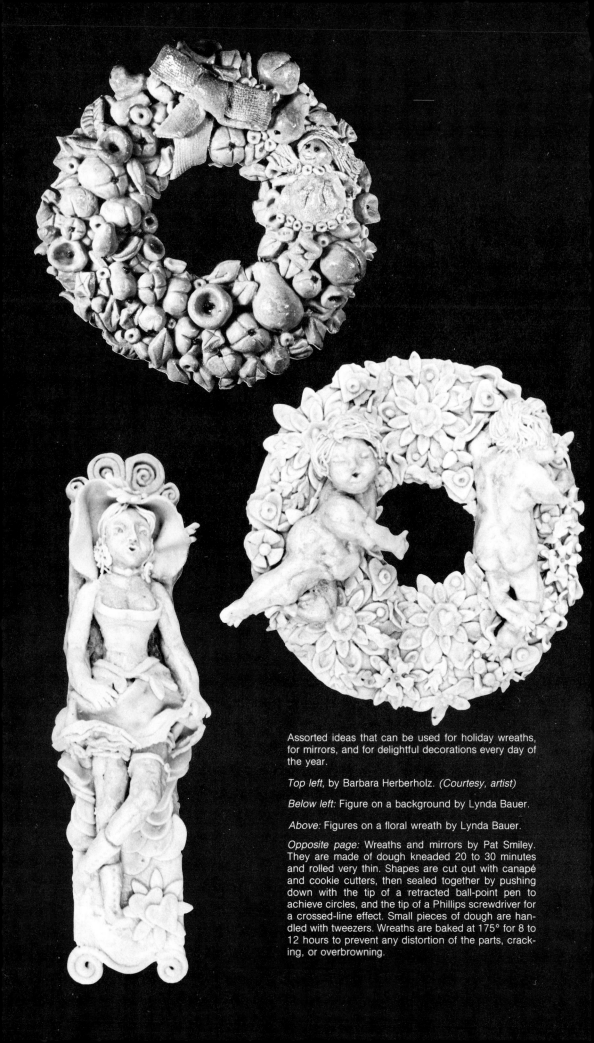

Assorted ideas that can be used for holiday wreaths, for mirrors, and for delightful decorations every day of the year.

Top left, by Barbara Herberholz. *(Courtesy, artist)*

Below left: Figure on a background by Lynda Bauer.

Above: Figures on a floral wreath by Lynda Bauer.

Opposite page: Wreaths and mirrors by Pat Smiley. They are made of dough kneaded 20 to 30 minutes and rolled very thin. Shapes are cut out with canapé and cookie cutters, then sealed together by pushing down with the tip of a retracted ball-point pen to achieve circles, and the tip of a Phillips screwdriver for a crossed-line effect. Small pieces of dough are handled with tweezers. Wreaths are baked at 175° for 8 to 12 hours to prevent any distortion of the parts, cracking, or overbrowning.

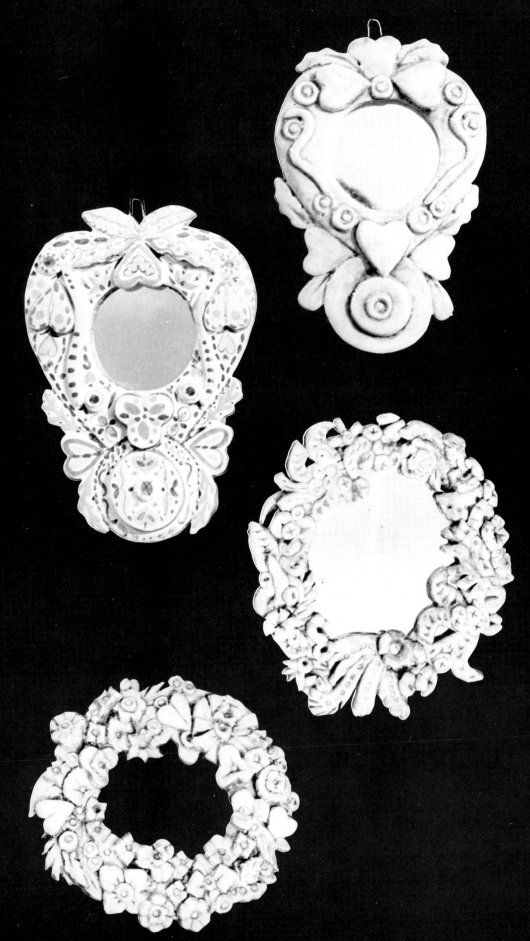

Suppliers of Specialty Items

Clock Parts
   Amaro & Sons, Department BD, 4888 Ronson Court, San Diego, California 92111 or sources listed in craft magazines

Dough-Art Tools
   Natcol Crafts, Inc., P.O. Box 299, Redlands, California 92373
   Lee Wards—local stores or Elgin, Illinois
   local craft shops

Paste Food Coloring and *Large-Tip Cake Decorators*
   Wilton Enterprises, 833 West 115th Street, Chicago, Illinois 60643. Also available from Sears Roebuck & Co. and Montgomery Ward houseware departments.

Index

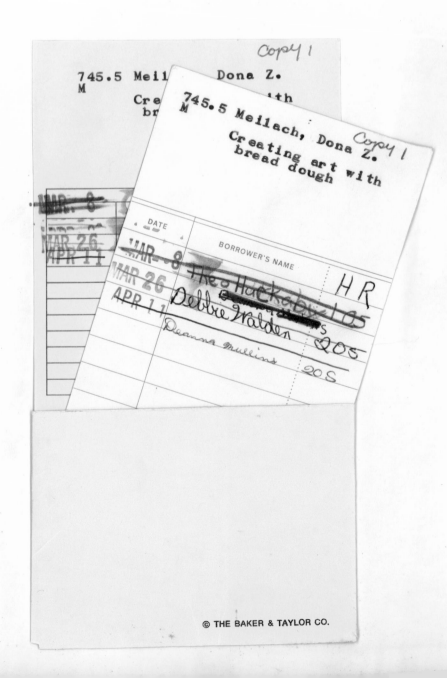